Dear Steve,

best wishes

Vinay

INVESTING FOR CHANGE

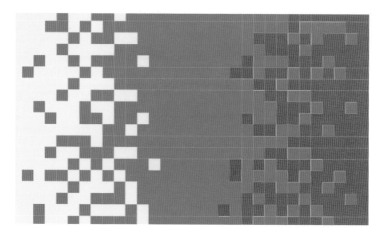

INVESTING FOR CHANGE

PROFIT FROM RESPONSIBLE INVESTMENT

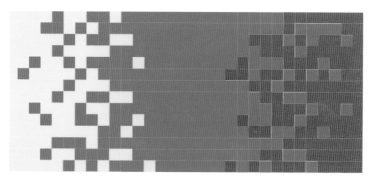

AUGUSTIN LANDIER AND VINAY B. NAIR

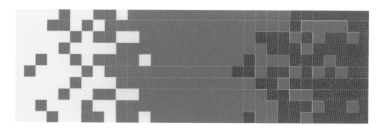

OXFORD
UNIVERSITY PRESS

2009

OXFORD
UNIVERSITY PRESS

Oxford University Press, Inc., publishes works that further
Oxford University's objective of excellence
in research, scholarship, and education.

Oxford New York
Auckland   Cape Town   Dar es Salaam   Hong Kong   Karachi
Kuala Lumpur   Madrid   Melbourne   Mexico City   Nairobi
New Delhi   Shanghai   Taipei   Toronto

With offices in
Argentina   Austria   Brazil   Chile   Czech Republic   France   Greece
Guatemala   Hungary   Italy   Japan   Poland   Portugal   Singapore
South Korea   Switzerland   Thailand   Turkey   Ukraine   Vietnam

Library of Congress Cataloging-in-Publication Data
Landier, Augustin.
Investing for change: profit from responsible investment / Augustin Landier, Vinay B. Nair.
    p.   cm.
Includes index.
ISBN 978-0-19-537014-0
1. Investments–Moral and ethical aspects.   I. Nair, Vinay B.
II. Title.
   HG4515.13.L36 2009
   332.6–dc22   2008012707

9 8 7 6 5 4 3 2 1

Printed in China
on acid-free paper

In the memory of Narayanan Balagopal and Nicolas Delvecchio

CONTENTS

INTRODUCTION

The Values Investor

In our lives, we play several roles regularly. We vote. We work. We buy things and services. And we invest.

Our money finds its way to companies through banks, mutual funds, pension funds, and—increasingly—direct trading. Every now and then, when an issue captures our attention, we contemplate our supporting or opposing roles as voters, as customers, and as employees. Seldom do we think of our roles as investors. Few ask why they invest in a different set of values from those they demand as customers, employees, or voters. In fact, few ask why they allow their investments to express a different set of values from those they expect family, friends, or colleagues to observe. But once the topic is raised, few feel indifferent to the issue of investing in corporations that hurt social well-being.

Despite its prevalence, investment is a remarkably impersonal activity. Undoubtedly, many investors find the inaccessibility of finance intimidating. That the profession is based on numbers is an important difficulty, for many people do not enjoy mathematics, and many find it complicated. This fact, combined with the specialized jargon involved in investments, forms a scary mixture that is both impersonal and intimidating.

Yet investors—if unconsciously—silently provide the fuel that keeps the world economy moving, unaware for the most part of the companies that use their savings.

This is now changing. Many investors now want their investments to reflect their values, and many have begun a journey to discover what their money is doing. We hope this book encourages many more. We hope it not only helps you think of the values your investments express but also shows how you can put your money to work for the changes you desire. For many people, giving significant money away for the purpose of promoting change is not a practical option. How would they meet their own needs? But investing for change is something many people can consider. As we argue in this book, in the case of many issues, investing for change—if done with financial acumen—adds to your personal wealth. You can now align your desire of making money with the kind of change you would like to see in the world.

This movement is often known as socially responsible investing (SRI), ethical investing, or simply responsible investing. Asset managers who together control about $11 trillion have indicated an interest in it—illustrating how attractive it has become.[1]

This mushrooming of interest in responsible investment did not occur overnight. The ingredients have been brewing for decades. In the United States, faith-based investors were avoiding ownership of financial assets that clashed with their faith as early as in the eighteenth century. In the second half of the twentieth century, endowments and public pension funds revived, in a secular manner, the idea of paying attention to the "values" in investing. This revival was strengthened by the shareholder activist movement, which gained momentum in the 1980s. The corporate governance changes that were made during this period were instrumental in allowing shareholders to express their views to managers and to exercise their rights as owners of companies. Rating companies and mutual funds also started taking into account companies' social behavior, making social investing more accessible to the public. Several individuals and institutions, with admirable zeal, played a critical role in bringing this movement to its present state.

The goals of the various responsible investors are different. And just as motives differ among people who opt for vegetarian food, motives differ among responsible investors. Moral vegetarians avoid meat for ethical reasons; they do not want to be accomplices in the killing of animals. Similarly, some investors avoid companies they believe are in the business of "sin."

For example, Guy, whom you will meet in chapter 2, wants to see his investments reflect his values. He wants nothing to do with certain products, including tobacco and alcohol.

Like a moral vegetarian who does not waver when the point is made that many others still eat meat, Guy does not make his investment decisions on the basis of whether his actions promote similar actions on the part of others or of corporations. And like moral vegetarians who may sometimes lose out on certain nutritional ingredients, Guy is also willing to sacrifice significant financial performance to achieve this goal. Let's call him a yellow investor. In the categorization we will present, the typical yellow investor approaches investing from the perspective of principles. Yellow investors want their portfolios to be exempt from "wrongly earned money." They don't want to be part of activities they disapprove of or from businesses they consider unethical. For this, they are willing to compromise financial performance. They believe that if everybody were to behave like them, such companies would go out of business. When reminded that not everyone does behave like them, they are unshaken.

Unlike moral vegetarians, health vegetarians avoid meat for practical reasons, like lowering cholesterol. There is a similar type of "more practical" values investor. Kathy, for example (introduced in chapter 1), wants to express her values in her investments, in order to promote these values in corporate actions and the economy. She also wants to make sure that doing so will not hurt her financial returns much. We will call Kathy's type the *blue* investor. **Blue** investors typically want to know how much it will cost them to invest responsibly, and whether it will ultimately have an impact. They are the more practical and less "ethical" of the responsible investors. If **blue** investors were persuaded that SRI would not affect the way companies behave or that its impact on their portfolio performance would be large, they would look for another way to participate in changing the world.

Ted (whom you will meet in chapter 4), unlike Kathy and Guy, has no interest in expressing his values through his portfolio per se. He is not a vegetarian at all! His only goal in investments is to generate higher returns and improve financial performance. It might then seem puzzling to some that he is interested in SRI, but he believes that through responsible investing he can generate superior financial performance. We call Ted's type *red* investors. **Red** investors' sole goal is to maximize returns. If that means being responsible, they will promote corporate responsibility. However, if that means ignoring social obligations, they support that, too. They are not "amoral" or cynical, but they usually express their values through other aspects of their lives.

Since you were intrigued enough to pick up this book, you probably have some interest in responsible investment. What are your goals and motives? What are the causes you strongly believe in and support—or oppose?

Chances are that for some of the issues you have thought about you are a yellow investor, for some others you might relate to **blue** investors, and for others you might agree with the **red** investors.

Here is a (very short) list of some issues. Which of these are your yellow issues? Which are your **blue** issues?

- Respect for human rights
- Better health-care benefits
- Higher safety standards for products
- Healthier food
- Democracy
- Lower carbon dioxide emissions
- Animal rights
- Banning sales of weapons to individuals in your country
- Avoiding sales of weapons to rogue regimes
- Not taking advantage of other people's addictions to nicotine, alcohol, or gambling
- Higher ethnic and gender diversity in corporate management
- Equal opportunity employment

When it comes to views about responsible investing, each investor is a built-in mixture of yellow, **blue**, and **red**, combining different motives and goals. As you read this book, you will see that some parts relate more naturally to your yellow issues, while some others relate more naturally to your **blue** or **red** issues.

We will return to your issues in chapter 6. We hope to provide you with a realistic idea of the promise and an assessment of the limitations that responsible investment holds with regard to an issue you care about.

INVESTING FOR CHANGE

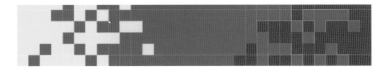

Investing to Express Your Values

▪▪▪▪ A Natural Idea

Kathy is on her way to an appointment with her financial advisor, Tim. As she scans the newspaper, a story grabs her attention. She reads:

> "Last week, we spent four days working from dawn until about one o'clock in the morning the following day. I was so tired I felt sick," he whispers, tears streaming down his face. "If any of us cried we were hit with a rubber pipe. Some of the boys had oily cloths stuffed in our mouths as punishment."[1]

The article is about a raid by Indian police on a sweatshop in the back streets of New Delhi. Ten-year-old children worked there, making hand-sewn clothes in inhumane conditions. While such child labor situations exist all over the developing world—including India—the news media have latched onto this story because the clothes are being made for a large retailer with a globally recognized brand—Gap Inc.

The article worries Kathy. She is concerned that the T-shirts she buys for her own children at the mall might also be produced in horrendous conditions by other children in other parts of the world. For Kathy, it is not enough just to feel sorry and do nothing; she sees inaction and indifference almost as forms of irresponsibility. Having achieved a certain degree of financial freedom, as she sees her children grow, she is more conscious about the impact her decisions have on others' lives. The small gestures she makes to avoid harming the environment make her feel better. Her actions, however small, to help others in her community and remote continents are deeply satisfying. The concept of "acting responsibly" is a source of harmony in Kathy's daily life. She believes her values define her as an individual, more than her lifestyle or career. That is why she contributes to nonprofit organizations and occasionally even volunteers. But as the Gap incident shows, companies can sometimes undo the good that many people like her attempt to do. After all, in 2007, of the 100 largest economic entities in the world, 32 are companies, not countries.

Gap Inc. was clearly embarrassed to be at the center of such a story, but sometimes, companies are not even embarrassed to be involved in such situations. Consider Petrochina: Worth more than a trillion dollars by the end of 2007, this Chinese oil company now has the largest market capitalization in the world. Its parent company, China National Petroleum Corp., is helping the Sudan government drill oil.

China National Petroleum owns 41% of Petrodar Operating, based in Khartoum, while Malaysia's state-owned Petroliam Nasional owns 40%, according to Petrodar's Web site. The venture opened a 1,400-kilometer, or 870-mile, pipeline last April to carry 200,000 barrels of oil a day from fields in the Melut Basin to Port Sudan on the Red Sea. China National

Petroleum started commercial production of the Dar Blend crude oil from its production-sharing field in Sudan last year. The field in southeastern Sudan will produce 200,000 barrels per day, it said.[2]

According to the Save Darfur Coalition and other advocacy groups, "the Sudanese government uses up to 70% of its oil revenues, generated mainly through foreign direct investment, to give arms and supplies to the Janjaweed militia accused of the killings in Darfur."[3] The conflict in Sudan's Darfur region has taken more than 200,000 lives and displaced some two and a half million people since rebels took up arms against the government in 2003. As early as January 2005, a report commissioned by the United Nations concluded that

> the Government of the Sudan and the Janjaweed are responsible for serious violations of international human rights and humanitarian law amounting to crimes under international law. In particular, the Commission found that Government forces and militias conducted indiscriminate attacks, including killing of civilians, torture, enforced disappearances, destruction of villages, rape and other forms of sexual violence, pillaging and forced displacement, throughout Darfur. These acts were conducted on a widespread and systematic basis, and therefore may amount to crimes against humanity.[4]

Going further than the UN report, in June 2005, President Bush said that the killings in Sudan's Darfur region constitute genocide.

By enabling the Sudan government to finance its military repression, companies like Petrochina arguably act against the efforts of the international community to stop the Darfur killings.

If you learned that through your mutual funds holdings, you are one of the many shareholders of Petrochina, would you care about it? And even if you sold your shares, would your actions change the way Petrochina does business?

Kathy now views her meeting with Tim from a different perspective. She had always wished she could *see more concretely what her savings are used for*: which companies get her money, and what do they do with it. The news story about the Gap has brought that desire to the forefront. Kathy believes the *values* she stands for and the *financial planning decisions* she has to make with her advisor Tim about her investments are *deeply connected*. She would find it natural to invest in companies that embrace her concerns—those that are striving to be more sensitive to the environment and demonstrate greater concern for the living standards of workers in poor countries. Kathy intuitively sees such investments both as a moral duty and as a vote that signals her approval of companies that are moving in the right direction. As her train approaches Manhattan, she resolves to raise these issues with Tim, even if her ideas about them are still a little unclear.

Questions swirl in her mind. Might it be possible to invest her savings in ways that reflect her values? Will Tim find her attitude too naïve? Is it possible to "express one's values" through one's investments? How easy is it to rank companies along standards of social rather than financial value? Wouldn't such standards be subjective? And what about financial performance? Would "SRI" imply taking more risks with her retirement savings? And what about the impact: Would it be worth the effort to channel one's *money* toward "virtuous companies"? Would it help them compete more vigorously with less socially responsible corporations? In political elections, the candidate who gets the most votes wins, so Kathy's choice makes a clear difference. But in the world of finance, will the investment choices she and others like her make be enough to force less virtuous companies to improve their behavior, or will they just seek out and find other sources of funding? She won't be the first to raise these questions with Tim. You might have thought about some of these questions yourself.

▪▪▪▪▪ Beyond the Liberal Model of Change

Kathy and you are not isolated examples; you represent a growing category of individuals who feels strongly about several core issue areas, including environment-friendliness and human rights. People in this group want all aspects of their lives, including investing, to be in harmony with their beliefs. They belong to a growing segment of American society that sociologist Paul H. Ray and psychologist Sherry R. Anderson described in 2000 as "cultural creatives":[5]

> These individuals are not exclusively guided by material and status achievements and their values embrace a strong interest in other people and care about the ecosystem. They number around 50 million in the U.S. today; that is one in six people. And this number is growing.

Many in this group feel that corporate behavior sometimes clashes with their values. According to a Gallup survey in December 2006, 65% of Americans said they would like to see "major corporations having less influence" (compared to only 52% in 2001). And only 18% said that they had "confidence in big business" (28% in 2001). Together, these polls suggest dissatisfaction with the way corporations conduct their business. This might suggest that people might demand more government control over corporations. However, only a third of the United States population believes that there is "too little regulation of business and industry." Interestingly, this shows that people don't view government intervention as the way to make large companies more responsible.

This is where Kathy differs from her parents. Both her parents were liberal professors. For them, free markets often meant the organized exploitation of the weak by the strong. Kathy, on the other hand, believes that profits and competition are powerful tools to motivate people. She believes that people driven by incentives can make society progress. For that reason, she realizes that big business will adopt a more socially responsible approach if it profits by doing so. Some 20 years ago, when she was still a student, she thought political activism was the way to pressure big business to do the right things for society. She would have fought for a tightening of laws and government controls on corporate behavior.

Today, Kathy is skeptical about that approach; in a global world, there is only so much that national governments can do. Regulation often takes time to reflect public opinion. In addition, companies also weigh in heavily on which laws are finally adopted. Companies react when a state passes regulations that are costly for them, such as higher environmental standards. If the impact on profits is high, they may relocate production centers and sometimes even headquarters to a more favorable location. In the United States, since the enforcement of the Clean Air Act in the early 1970s, polluting industries have relocated over time to the counties that had the lowest regulatory constraints (those for which the Clean Air Act requirements were not binding).[6] This relocation had a large cost for local economies. According to Michael Greenstone, an economist based at the Massachusetts Institute of Technology, due to such relocations, "in the first 15 years in which the Clean Air Act was in force (1972–87), nonattainment counties (relative to attainment ones) lost approximately 590,000 jobs, $37 billion in capital stock, and $75 billion (1987 dollars) of output in pollution-intensive industries."[7]

Now more than before, companies can threaten to move because in the era of globalization, transportation and communication costs are low. Labor also tends to be cheaper in less developed countries, which typically have lax regulation. This relocation threat is something politicians take into account in their political agendas: Such relocations, leading to plant closures, are by nature unpopular and decrease politicians' chances of being reelected.

Moreover, industries that are most affected by regulation organize in powerful lobbies that try to influence the making of laws by financing political parties and campaigning to shape public opinion. The pharmaceutical industry provides an example of such powerful industrial lobbying.

Drug companies spent more on lobbying than any other industry between 1998 and 2005—$900 million, according to the nonpartisan Center for Responsive Politics. They donated a total of $89.9 million in the same period to federal candidates and party committees, nearly three-quarters of it to Republicans.... The industry worked closely with the Republican Congress to shape the Medicare prescription drug program, which included a provision barring the government from negotiating with the pharmaceutical industry for lower prices. In the three-year run-up to passage, industry lobbyists poured more than $6 million into both Republican and Democratic campaign coffers, dispatched an army of more than 800 lobbyists to Capitol Hill and quietly funded seniors organizations and patient advocacy groups that opposed Democratic alternatives.[8]

Political Economy: Game Theory Applied to Government and Regulation

Game theory is the science of strategic behavior. Using the framework developed by the mathematician John Nash, it studies how rational, self-interested players should act in different contexts. The economist Mancur Olson, a pioneer of modern political economy, borrowed from game theory to model the formation of laws and institutions. In his *Theory of Collective Action* (1965), Olson builds on the fact that governments are not purely altruistic bodies and can be influenced by special interests. He provides a simple explanation for why regulations that emerge from the political game are not necessarily the best for the collective good. Industries invest in the formation of lobbies that influence regulation in their favor. Since the benefits of these favorable regulations are concentrated among a few companies while the costs are shared by the whole population, game theory predicts that there will be little public resistance to them. Indeed, if they were to put effort in changing these regulations, citizens would only get a tiny fraction of the total benefits of change so they have little individual incentive to invest in such political activism. This effect is called the free-rider problem in game theory.

Kathy realized that no matter how much the public may agree on certain views, it takes time for them to become laws. She remembered how successful the tobacco lobby had been in delaying legislation on tobacco commercials: The ban on cigarette commercials only became effective in 1971, even though consensus on the health hazard of cigarettes emerged much earlier. The ban was instituted seven years after the Advisory Committee to the Surgeon General issued a unanimous report stating that "cigarette smoking is causally related to lung cancer" and "is a health hazard of sufficient importance in the United States to warrant appropriate remedial action."

Kathy believes that in cases like the New Delhi sweatshop, acting as a shareholder might be faster and more effective than acting as a citizen. From her own experience working in corporate America, she knows that companies sometimes act in ways that are legal but that she would find morally unacceptable. On the other hand, she also knows that companies often undertake social initiatives though they are not legally obliged to do so.

Do you believe, like Kathy, that regulation is not the only way to influence the behavior of companies? If so, your choices as an investor might be a meaningful way to express your values.

Gary Matthews, a financial advisor with First Affirmative Financial Network, has said: "in general, I think Paul Ray's research on 'cultural creatives' accurately describes potential SRI clients as a group: people who care deeply about ecology and saving the planet, about relationships, peace and social justice, and about self actualization, spirituality and self-expression. In my opinion there is a market of 30 million to 40 million people in the U.S. who would be SRI clients if they knew that SRI existed."[9]

▯▯▮▮▮ **Values around the World: You Are Not Alone**

Halfway around the world from Kathy's train, in India, Ravi is heading home after a full day of work at Bangalore's information technology center. Wages have grown exponentially for top engineers like Ravi, who now makes a comfortable $60,000 a year.

The Boom of Indian "Super-Haves"

A 2006 survey by global consultants KPMG said in India there were about 30–40 million "Super-Haves" (people with an annual income of over $30,000). According to a 2006 American Express survey, the cumulative liquid wealth of affluent Indians is projected to grow 59% from $203 billion in 2006 to $322 billion by 2009. The survey shows how rapidly the affluent Indian population is growing. Currently there are 711,000 people in India who have liquid wealth of $100,000 or more. This number is expected to reach 1.1 million by 2009. In 2005, India already had about 83,000 millionaires (with assets of more than $1 million). The millionaire pool is expected to expand by 12.8% annually, the report said.[10]

Ravi hears the news on his car radio about the sweatshop raid involving the Gap. He knows how privileged his life has been in comparison to these children's lives.

Kathy and Ravi have more in common than the fact that they are hardworking executives. Their core values are strikingly similar, though they are both deeply rooted, culturally and emotionally, in their respective countries. They have different religious beliefs and enjoy different cuisines. Yet they share several values. They both feel revolted by violence among humans; they believe political regimes that do not respect human rights should be under pressure to change; they consider pollution and environment preservation to be serious issues for which their generation will be collectively accountable.

It is hardly surprising that they both believe that business organizations should care about their impact on society and the environment. As a result, the Gap news story has a similar effect on both of them. Essentially, they both tend to be outraged by many of the same things. What makes the core values of Kathy and Ravi so much more similar than, say, their grandfathers'? First, Kathy and Ravi form many of their views on the basis of information from similar sources. Countries today trade cultural goods more intensely than ever. This goes beyond Hollywood movies and soap operas. More and more people have access to global media. They use international news channels and the internet to obtain information, and accordingly, their perceptions of the world are more similar than used to be the case. Little wonder that the educated middle class is converging in several core values.

But what makes Ravi and Kathy pay attention to the same news story? What makes them both visit CNN and BBC? The similarity of their aspirations also stems from their access to education and their freedom from material constraints. This makes them think about and pay attention to similar issues. The convergence has little to do with the fact that both Kathy and Ravi drink Coca-Cola or that clothing habits and hairstyles are now converging all over the world. Apart from their consumption habits, the way they spend their leisure hours is remarkably different. Ravi watches television when he returns from work, while Kathy does not even own a television set. Ravi is a fan of rap; Kathy prefers classical music. What they share is having reached a level of wealth that frees them from thinking about survival. In this sense, common core values are not the result of the domination of one culture over another but the natural development of the potential of humankind.

Consider this evidence: Every year, the World Values Survey asks households in more than 80 countries to answer several questions. The survey provides a unique insight into values and attitudes among the world population. Questions address issues ranging from religious beliefs to opinions about free trade. Unsurprisingly, opinions and attitudes vary widely across countries. For example, 82% of the Bangladesh population believe "divorce is never justifiable," while only 2% of Swedes agree with this statement. Some 81% of people surveyed in the United

States believe in life after death, but only 16% in Vietnam do. For 69% of the Japanese, "television is the most important form of entertainment"; only 33% of Canadians agree.

Despite this wide disparity in global opinions, one clear pattern emerges from the responses to the survey. As societies become more affluent, they experience a *migration of values*. As constraints on persons' existence are relaxed as a result of economic growth, there appears to be a shift away from "materialist" values, emphasizing economic and physical security, and toward "postmaterialist" values, emphasizing self-expression and quality-of-life concerns."[11]

Interestingly, *all* societies experience such a shift as they grow economically. Regardless of their culture or religion, individuals in developing societies express less submission to authority and have a stronger desire to express their views than those in societies that are not developing. They have a stronger concern for the quality of life. A growing emphasis on environmental protection and rising demands for participation in decision making in economic and political life are a feature of economic development. As Ronald Inglehart and Christian Welzel have said, "this cultural shift is found throughout postindustrial society."[12]

Luckily, increasing wealth does not make humans more "selfish." While it makes people more autonomous in their opinions, it also gives them an opportunity to think beyond their own lives. Freed of the need to struggle for survival, we humans become both self-expressive and socially concerned. Inglehart and Welzel show that these changes are pronounced between generations.

Generations experiencing higher levels of material wealth than their parents migrate toward "postmaterialism." Ravi and Kathy belong to such a generation, benefiting from tremendous economic developments in the United States over the past three decades.

Postmaterialist Values and Individual Characteristics: Results from the World Values Survey

The World Values Survey contains two indices, based on the work of social scientists Inglehart and Welzel, that measure "postmaterialist values" and "self-expression values" for each individual.[13] Let's define individuals in the top 50% of these respective indices as "self-expressive" and "postmaterialist." The probability of an individual being a "postmaterialist" and being "self-expressive" both increase significantly with income and education level and decrease with age. A 1% increase in the per capita gross domestic product of a country increases by 10% a citizen's probability of being "postmaterialist" and by 4% a citizen's probability of being "self-expressive."[14]

Along with wealth, proximity to social harm also has an influence on people's level of concern about social and environmental issues. A person who grew up exposed to pollution and human rights violations is more likely to be socially concerned about these issues than someone who did not. For this reason, as the number of wealthy individuals increases in developing countries such as India and China, capital is likely to become more compassionate than before.

The rise of "cultural creatives" has now become a worldwide phenomenon. The fact that wealth and education are strong determinants of "postmaterialist values" suggests that these values and thus the potential scope of SRI are spreading in the world.

▪▪▪▪▪ **The Wealth of the Planet**

As more countries today get access to education and a chance to develop, the number of people who care about postmaterialist values and have a strong desire to express them is growing substantially. Young generations in developing countries are becoming wealthier, more "concerned," and more numerous than their parents' generation. This means that the potential market for SRI is growing.

Take, for example, a specific "value": concern for the environment. The World Values Survey asks people if they would be willing to "give part of their income if certain that the money would be used to reduce environmental pollution." It is likely that individuals who strongly agree with this statement would care about the environmental policy of the companies in which they invest. They are good candidates for SRI. Not surprisingly, people with high incomes are more likely to answer yes to this question. The survey also shows that the highly educated are 15% more likely to answer yes than those who have little education. Another striking fact is that the more highly educated people in poor countries are more prone to answer yes than their counterparts in rich countries. It is indeed the case that individual capital, while being smaller, is more compassionate in poorer countries. This is probably because the effects of pollution on daily life are more acute and obvious in these countries.[15] If emerging countries keep on growing at the speed of the last decade, SRI could have large margins of expansion in these economies.

While the number of concerned investors will indeed grow, it will remain a small minority of the world's population for some time to come. According to the World Bank, approximately 50% of the world population still lives in conditions of struggling to meet basic needs. This group consists of approximately 2.5 billion people who survive on less than $2 a day—a category often termed relative poverty.[16] Clearly, this large group is far from being investors, let alone concerned investors. Suggesting otherwise would be absurd.

So only a minority of the world population can practice SRI, yet they claim that it has great power. The explanation of this seeming contradiction lies in the fact that, as noted, those who "care" tend to be those who have secured their own material future and have financial wealth to invest. So a minority of concerned individuals control a disproportionately larger share of the investments. The world's wealth lies in the hands of a few people. According to a report published by the World Institute for Development Economics Research, and based on data from 2000, the top 2% of the world's population owns more than half the world's wealth, and the top 10% owns 85%.[17] It is the growing concern about social issues among this minority that makes SRI important and relevant.

> ### Fat Tails: The Disproportionate Importance of the Biggest
>
> For many phenomena in nature and society, the largest individuals of the population account for a disproportionately large fraction of the total size. Statisticians refer to this notion as "fat tail distributions." This "fat tail" effect holds for phenomena as different as the size of cities, the frequency at which we use words when we speak, the number of connections to websites, and financial wealth. The Italian economist Vilfredo Pareto (1828–1943) observed that 80% of income in Italy went to 20% of the population. His result is known in common language as the "80–20 rule," which states that for many events, 80% of the effect comes from 20% of the causes. Currently, in the United States, the top 10% of the population, ranked by income, earns some 42% of the country's total income.[18]

The future of the SRI movement hinges on the desire of the wealthiest individuals of the planet to use their investments to improve the world. The good news is that this desire exists.

An analogy can be drawn with philanthropy. The grants that are allocated to not-for-profit projects are very largely determined by the choices of the richest individuals and the foundations they back. The fact they are totally free from the concern of securing their own material comfort leads many of these individuals to "give back" large fractions of their wealth. According to the *Chronicle of Philanthropy*, a newspaper that covers the nonprofit world, "for the 112 philanthropies that reported data for the 2005 and 2006 fiscal years, the Bill and Melinda Gates Foundation, with $33-billion in assets, remains the wealthiest grant maker in the nation. If Gates's assets were excluded from the *Chronicle*'s survey, the total wealth for the remaining 111 foundations would fall 18% to $152.4-billion. Gates is almost assured of continuing its reign as number 1, thanks to a $36.1-billion pledge from the investor Warren E. Buffett."[19] In June 2006, the second richest man on the planet after Bill Gates, legendary investor Warren Buffett, announced he was giving most of his wealth to the foundation set up by Bill Gates and his wife, Melinda. The total assets of the Gates Foundation alone are expected to reach $100 billion before the end of the decade. So a small number of people are determining the allocation of the bulk of the money being given.

▨▨■■ Early Adopters

Whether many of these "caring investors" ultimately express their values through their investments or through other means will depend on whether they believe that SRI *is actually an effective way to change the world*. At the same time, whether SRI makes a difference or not depends on how many people practice it. If it remains a very small minority, companies can afford to ignore the responsible investor's voice. In that case, SRI will have little impact.

It is a Catch-22. If the success of a new idea depends on the number of people who accept it, there is a risk that nobody will adopt it precisely because nobody has already done so. So the innovation never takes off. We see many examples of such ideas in our lives—only the successful ones. For example, when Sony and Phillips introduced the compact disc (CD) in 1981, no one knew whether the switch from vinyl to digital would happen. Customers thought they would start buying CDs only when all kinds of music were available in retail stores in this format. Meanwhile, music distributors thought they would increase the supply of CDs in stores only when enough customers were willing to buy them.

Fortunately for the CD mavens, large numbers of enthusiastic "early adopters" began switching to CDs. They were sufficiently intrigued by the new technology to ignore the risk that it wouldn't become a standard. This critical mass of early enthusiasts was enough to convince distributors and "skeptical customers" to switch. The rest is history; CDs became the standard music medium for decades.

Is the same kind of development likely with SRI? Do enough early adopters exist to boost the appeal of SRI for others? As we write, the answer is yes. Several SRI products have been launched, and they are not in danger of disappearing. Even if Tim, Kathy's financial advisor, turns out to be a "skeptical customer," he won't tell her that her desire is just a fantasy. Investing responsibly *is* possible, and millions of individuals have already adopted the practice, putting billions of dollars to work. The Social Investment Forum reports that at the end of 2005, in the United States, SRI involved nearly $2.3 trillion— 10% of the assets under management in the United States. This represents an annual growth rate of 25% in the 1995–2005 decade, slightly higher than the growth of assets under management in the United States.

Who were these early enthusiasts? Why did they make the choice to practice SRI when there were concerns that it might not have a significant impact, even that such investing might hurt portfolio returns?

Thou Shalt Not Profit from Evil

As noted, SRI's origins can be traced back to early faith-based initiatives. In the eighteenth century, the Quakers avoided investments in weapons, casinos, alcohol, and polluting industries such as tanning. John Wesley, one of the founders of the Methodist church, formulated the doctrine that it is immoral to profit from activities that hurt one's neighbor.

Many of today's SRI funds are inheritors of this doctrine. For people who practice faith-based SRI, the fact that avoiding "vice industries" might not change the world—as these businesses might find other investors—is not critical in their decision. Faith-driven investors believe they are morally accountable for the behavior of the companies they finance. In accordance with this faith-based origin of the movement, the first modern socially responsible mutual fund, Pax World, was created in 1971 by two Methodist ministers. Today, Pax World still invests in companies that meet positive standards of responsibility and manages $2.6 billion in assets for more than 100,000 investors.

Institutional Capital: The Values of the Public

The movement rapidly extended to funds managed by secular but conscious groups such as cities, states, colleges, and public pension funds. What do these institutions have in common that led them to become early adopters of SRI?

Part of the answer lies in the people who contribute to these institutions. Money in an educational institution's endowment might come from an alumna giving back to her alma mater. For such an investor, the funds have a charitable aspect. A public pension fund might be managing retirement money for public school teachers and other state employees. For such contributors, the funds are a bit like taxed money. Imagine that the fund that provides retirement benefits for California public employees makes an extra 1% return. Given the size of the fund, that would represent a not-so-meager $2.5 billion. Where would this extra money go?

It would not be paid directly to the 1.5 million public employees who contribute to the fund, because they are paid a predetermined retirement benefit based on the defined benefits contract. This makes these contributors less concerned about the fund's returns; as long as it doesn't go bankrupt, its financial performance is not a major issue for them. The enhanced performance will mostly benefit future generations of workers, since superior fund performance will allow them to contribute less for a similar level of benefits—so in a sense, the additional money belongs to "future generations." This makes it natural for the present contributors to be sensitive to the possibility of the fund's investment policy reflecting their values. And as a rule, people don't like their tax money or charitable funds to finance causes they don't believe in.

Likes and dislikes, however, stem from information. That public pension funds and universities are subject to high standards of transparency (by regulation or by demand) serves to make their contributors informed. Consequently, the average investor is conscious of the "message" these holdings convey. If the message is purely about "greed and profits," public outrage usually follows. Just as nonfinancial constituents don't want public institutions to have missions that fail to reflect their values, financial contributors don't want public money to be associated with commonly scorned values. In that spirit, former California governor Jerry Brown used to say that the trustees of public investment funds should be "the conscience of California" and use the holdings to vote against unethical or unsocial corporate behavior.

Russell Sparkes, a fund manager who specializes in SRI, shows in his book *Socially Responsible Investment: A Global*

Revolution how public opinion has forced U.S. public investment funds to take ethical aspects into consideration. For example, South Africa at the time was an apartheid regime that oppressed black citizens. The University of Wisconsin divested South-Africa related companies "following a period of constant campus unrest and a legal opinion from the Wisconsin State Attorney General."[20] In 1983, all Massachusetts funds similarly divested. The following year, pension funds from New York and California adopted strict guidelines on the South Africa issue. Several major public pension funds and academic endowments across the United States joined the movement: "By the mid-1980s, seven states [and] 28 cities…had enacted divestment proposals. Forty-three educational institutions had fully or partially divested."[21]

This issue for the first time forced many reluctant investment managers to pay attention to values in their portfolios. Their reluctance diminished as they began to see the impact. SRI enthusiasts often describe the South Africa campaign as the first large, defining battle the movement won. "Between 1984 and May 1990, 206 US companies had partially or completely withdrawn from South Africa.… The progressive financial community and the major church institutions in America combined forces and unleashed a powerful 'corporate campaign.'"[22] Progressively, the public outrage about the involvement of large U.S. companies in the South Africa situation took over, and the notion that shareholders had a role to play in convincing companies to change became common wisdom that extended beyond faith-based capital and into institutional and public capital.

The South Africa campaign shaped the SRI movement and attracted public attention to the power shareholders could wield in nonfinancial matters. In Europe, the Ethical Investment Research Service was created in 1983 to respond to churches' demand for information on corporate involvements in South

Africa. Acknowledging the importance of the movement, many corporations started in this period to engage in dialogue with large institutional shareholders about the social and environmental impact of their policies. Many others began to publicize information about these topics.

The conversion of public pension funds and university endowments to SRI was a crucial step toward giving the movement a "faith-neutral" dimension, by defining a secular notion of "social injury."[23] For example, the proxy voting guidelines of the California State Teacher Pension Fund adopted in 1978 define "social injury" as existing when "the activities of a corporation serve to undermine basic human rights or dignities."

▪▪▪▪▪ **Current Adopters**

Today, with its secular identity well established, the SRI movement is more alive than ever. The Social Investment Forum reported that at the end of 2005, in the United States, SRI involved nearly $2.3 trillion—10% of assets under management in the United States. Of the $2.3 trillion, $0.7 trillion are in active funds that bring their social and environmental concerns to managements' attention rather than simply staying away from investing in these companies. This share of active capital had increased by 57% since 2003.

A good way to keep abreast of the evolution of the SRI market, is to consult the website of the Social Investment Forum (the U.S. SRI industry association, financed by more than 500 institutions), www.socialinvest.org. This website posts valuable information and frequent updates on industry trends. The website of the forum's "sister" organization in Europe is www.eurosif .org. (Specifically for the United Kingdom, one can consult www .uksif.org).

Among institutional SRI clients, public pension funds are the dominant investors. Approximately $1.2 trillion of public pension fund assets are invested according to an SRI framework that takes into account companies' impacts on their social and natural environments. This $1.2 trillion is roughly 45% of total state and local pension holdings.

The high-growth segment of SRI assets in the United States is mutual fund assets. About 200 mutual funds with social screens held $179 billion in 2005. This is still a small fraction (less than 2%) of the $10 trillion of assets in U.S. mutual funds, leaving ample room for future growth. (If Kathy were to decide to adopt SRI, this is where her money would go. Ravi could also invest in overseas funds but is hoping to see many more such options in his own country.) With 200 socially responsible mutual funds, this segment of SRI assets has increased fifteenfold since 1995.

Many mutual funds now allow individual investors to invest in SRI products. For example, since March 2000, Teachers Insurance and Annuity Association, College Retirement Equities Fund (TIAA-CREF), one of the giants of the mutual funds industry, has offered investors a socially responsible option, CREF Social Choice. This fund had some $9 billion in net assets and more than 430,000 individual investors as of March 2007, making it the largest socially responsible portfolio in the United States. "We continue to see increasing demand for socially responsible investments from our clients and the broader market place.... We are very pleased to offer interested clients options that allow them to further align their investments with their values," Herb Allison, chief executive officer (CEO) of TIAA-CREF, declares.[24] These responsible mutual fund options are utilized by many employees who allocate part of their wages for retirement. In fact, about 19% of defined contribution plans offer an SRI option.[25]

Defined Benefits versus Defined Contributions Plans

In a 401(k) retirement plan, participating employees have a portion of their wage allocated to an individual account, and can choose where this money is invested from a list of available mutual funds. Such plans are called *defined contributions* plans, as the employer agrees on the amount to be invested while the employee works at the company.

By contrast, in a *defined benefits* plan, the employer agrees on the final annual amount or "pension" to be received by the employee after retirement. For that purpose, the employer allocates money to a private pension fund that is in charge of investing and managing risk so that the employer's commitments can be honored in the future.

Since 1980, significant changes have occurred in the kind of employment-based retirement plan U.S. private sector workers participate in. According to the Employee Benefit Research Institute, "Defined benefit plans have declined (reflecting pressures on defined benefit plan sponsors to control costs and funding volatility, in addition to increased regulatory burdens), while defined contribution (401(k)-type) plans have grown."[26] This trend favors SRI, as the inclusion of a responsible option in a 401(k) is not legally controversial: employees can choose whether or not to invest in that specific fund.

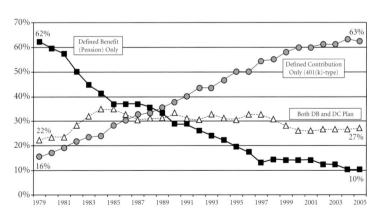

Figure 1.1 Retirement Plan Trends: Participation by Plan Type.
Source: U.S. Department of Labor, *Form 5500 Summary Report* (Summer 2004); ESRI estimates for 2002–2005.

The View from Europe

As is clear from its growing popularity in Europe, despite different regulation and institutions, SRI is a worldwide phenomenon. According to 2006 European SRI study published by the European Social Investment Forum (EUROSIF), SRI assets under management in Europe reached 1.03 trillion by 2005. The growth of the SRI market between 2003 and 2006 was 106%. During this period, European stocks grew at a rate of 70%, so the real growth of SRI assets was an impressive 36%.

As in the United States, most (94%) of these assets are from institutional clients, and the highest growth has come from mutual funds. "European SRI mutual funds won new business in the year to June 30, 2007 worth 43% more than the previous year, taking total assets to .49 billion," according to figures compiled by Morningstar and the SRI research company Vigeo Italia.[27]

Pension regulation in European countries has been a major driver of SRI growth. The UK was a pioneer, with its 1999 socially responsible pension fund regulation, which obliges all English pension funds to explain how they take social and environmental factors into account in their investment and voting decisions. The regulation states that trustees must write in their statement of investment principles their policy concerning "(a) the extent (if any) to which social, environmental or ethical considerations are taken into account in the selection, retention and realization of investments; and (b) their policy (if any) in relation to the exercise of the rights (including voting rights) attached to investments."[28] One of the law's goals was to clarify the legality of SRI-oriented pension funds' investment policies.

Several countries (e.g., Italy, Germany, Austria, and France) have followed the UK example by passing laws that give pension funds incentives to take values into account. For example, in

France, a 2001 law requires employee savings plans to specify in their internal rules the social, environmental, and ethical considerations they must take into account; and their annual reports must explain how this was done. A second law passed in 2001 requires the Retirement Reserve Fund (a .16 billion fund set up to support the French pension system) to report how their investment policy takes social, environmental, and ethical considerations into account.

Such transparency rules have helped resolve debates about whether the fiduciary obligations of pension funds—that is, their duties to act in the interest of their current and future beneficiaries—are compatible with SRI. In the United States, there is more controversy about this issue.

Private pension funds are subject to the federal Employee Retirement Income Security Act of 1974 (ERISA), which makes financial performance the exclusive goal of their investment policy. The Act requires that these funds invest "solely in the interest of plan participants and beneficiaries" and "for the exclusive purpose of providing benefits" to them. For a U.S. private pension fund, SRI is ERISA-compliant if the case can be made that it improves or at minimum does not deteriorate the financial characteristics of the plan's investment. The problem with private pension funds is that beneficiaries usually cannot choose how their money is managed and might disagree with some of the responsibility criteria used by the fund. This choice issue is solved in 401(k) plans, as plan participants can freely choose among different options, some of which can be socially responsible. In 1998, Calvert, one of the largest socially responsible mutual funds families, asked the Department of Labor to clarify whether offering a responsible option in a 401(k) plan would constitute a violation of ERISA rules. The Department replied that as long as it does not lead to inferior financial performance, SRI funds are a valid option in 401(k) plans.[29]

Sovereign Funds

Recently, other large institutional players have entered the SRI fray—sovereign wealth funds, which manage part of a country's national reserves. These funds act like giant national pension funds and manage money for nationwide retirement systems or simply hold the reserves of capital from national central banks. As you can guess, these funds are huge. For example, Norway has accumulated reserves of more than $350 billion in its Government Pension Fund. This fund is committed to avoiding investments that "may contribute to unethical acts or omissions, such as violations of fundamental humanitarian principles, serious violations of human rights, gross corruption or severe environmental damages." This mandate endorses universal values, independent of Norwegian culture. Gro Nystuen, a chairman of an ethics council screening the fund's investment, has said: "Inevitably, Norwegians feel bad about having all this money. Our job is to make the Norwegian people feel less guilty."[30]

Because of its size and credibility, this fund's decisions to divest a given company because of a social policy failure have received much public attention. For example, when the fund blacklisted Wal-Mart in 2006 (because of child labor and union obstruction issues) and sold $400 million worth of Wal-Mart shares, Wal-Mart's level of social responsibility was scrutinized in the media.

The UN Principles for Responsible Investment

Another milestone in the global growth of SRI, these principles, an investor initiative in partnership with the UN Environment Programme Finance Initiative and the UN Global Compact (see www.unpri.org), were published in 2006. Their purpose is the establishment of a common ground for SRI and to define a set of universal values and guidelines around which investors can organize their decisions. As of January 2008, financial services firms managing more than $10 trillion in assets had subscribed to the Principles for Responsible Investment. They are not region-specific and include all sizes and type of investors. As an indicator of current interest in SRI, this is a very encouraging sign.

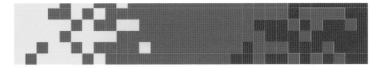

Can SRI Achieve Change?

 Making a Difference

Mkaya was already a "socially responsible investor" when he started using Tim as his financial advisor. Mkaya's background—he was from a South African family that had migrated to the United States—had forced him to follow one of SRI's early successes.

When many cities, states, colleges, faith-based groups, and pension funds throughout the United States began removing their investments from companies operating in South Africa, due to their opposition to apartheid, the decline in investment eventually forced a group of businesses, representing 75% of South African employers, to draft a charter calling for an end to apartheid. While efforts by socially responsible investors alone did not bring an end to apartheid, they did focus persuasive international pressure on the South African business community. At that time, this was just one of the few feathers in the cap of SRI; but it made a deep impression on Mkaya.

For every investor like Mkaya, many more among Tim's clients have their doubts about the value of SRI. Take, for example, Sven. Tim knows that Sven cares about expressing his values. He donates 10% of his income to charity—and not just because he wants the tax deductions. Tim once gently pointed out to Sven that his actions as a philanthropist were not consistent with his actions as an investor.

"Are you concerned that your investment portfolio does not reflect any of your social values?" Sven answered, matter-of-factly, "No." Tim remembers Sven's argument: "My portfolio decisions are unlikely to make any difference. When I express my voice through a donation, I know that it reaches the ear I want it to. But if I were to express my voice through my portfolio, my voice would be lost."

Sven *is* just one of many investors; and he is not a large investor. But he is underestimating his power as a shareholder. In this chapter, we will present several examples of companies that have begun to behave in socially responsible ways because their shareholders have voted with their investment dollars to encourage such behavior. Companies have implemented better corporate governance procedures, become more responsible stewards of the environment, and become more transparent about the ways their contractors treat workers—and these changes have come about because of pressure from socially responsible investors.

▊▊▊▆▆   The Corporate Governance Movement

Corporate governance—the ways corporations and corporate managers are governed—changed dramatically during the 1980s and 1990s. In the United States, for example, before 1980, corporate governance was, for all practical purposes, toothless. The mechanisms associated with governance were largely inactive. Corporate managers staffed boards with friends and family members. Executives were rarely fired, and life was quiet for the American CEO. He—and it was usually he—could run the company as he liked, and usually did.

During the 1980s, things began to change. Professors Steven Kaplan (University of Chicago) and Bengt Holmstrom (MIT) write:

> In the early 1980s, the wedge between actual and potential corporate performance became increasingly apparent. In some cases, changes in markets, technology, or regulation led to a large amount of excess capacity—for example, in the oil and tire industries. In others, it became apparent that diversification strategies carried out in the late '60s and '70s were underperforming. The top managers of such companies, however, were slow to respond to opportunities to increase value.... At the same time many U.S. companies were failing to maximize value, the U.S. capital markets were becoming more powerful because of increased stock ownership by large institutions.[1]

Lured by the desire to close the gap between potential and actual performance of corporations, large shareholders began to pressure managements to improve or leave. This activism was marked by hostility toward incumbent management, which was unusual in the corporate landscape at the time. Corporate raiders like Carl Icahn and T. Boone Pickens became household names, and terms such as "greenmail" and "LBO" (leveraged buyout) began to appear in newspaper headlines. Nearly half of all major U.S. corporations received a takeover offer in the 1980s. This awakened many CEOs from their slumber and forced them to restructure their firms in order to improve their performance.

During the 1990s, shareholders found a more balanced role: Rather than buying a whole company and replacing the management, they began to use their rights as shareholders to influence corporate policy and appeal to the board to get problems fixed. The hostile takeover tide of the 1980s began to ebb. Managers were more likely to be replaced through dismissal rather than a takeover. Other governance channels—such as performance-based pay and executive dismissal—became more powerful. Detecting this trend, Monks and Minnow started a fund in 1992 that invested in well-governed companies.

Over the course of that decade, shareholder-friendly companies outperformed their management-friendly counterparts by almost 90%.

Recognizing Good Corporate Governance

Companies with high standards of corporate governance function more like democracies than dictatorships. Managers are appointed and removed on the basis of their performance. The company is not ruled by an imperial CEO immune to criticism.

For such democratic governance, companies need several mechanisms that can provide checks and balances. For instance, most of the board should consist of independent directors with no ties to the management. These directors should have significant financial holdings in the company, so that their interests are aligned with the shareholders', and they should be appointed in a democratic way. The process through which the board gets elected should be formally encoded in a company's by-laws, the equivalent of a constitution for a country. In several well-known U.S. companies, a minority of shareholders (such as a controlling family or the managers themselves) have special shares with multiple voting rights—a system of "dual citizenship" that is considered a "lack of democracy," as it allows a few shareholders to go against the will of the majority. Another example: The by-laws of several large U.S. companies state that "the board of directors shall be divided into three classes of directors serving staggered three-year terms." This rule is considered "antidemocratic" because it prevents shareholders from removing a majority of the board in less than two years.

Several corporate governance rating agencies look at such mechanisms and give a corporate governance grade to a company.[2]

More recently, scandals at companies such as Enron and WorldCom have further strengthened the corporate governance movement. The consequences of misreporting information to shareholders have been dire—as was illustrated in the high-profile trials of Enron and WorldCom CEOs.

New legislation has lent more meaning to shareholder meetings. The New York Stock Exchange and the National Association of Securities Dealers Automated Quotation System have required, since 2003, that the boards of companies listed on their exchanges have majorities of independent directors. In the United States, the Sarbanes-Oxley Act has increased boards of directors' accountability. Internal controls are now the direct responsibility of directors. Facing greater liability, boards have become more receptive to the voices of shareholders.

Recent academic research gives evidence of this receptivity. Diane Del Guercio, Laura Wallis, and Tracie Woidtke of the University of Oregon and the University of Tennessee studied the effects of "vote no" campaigns, in which some active shareholders try to convince others, via letters, press releases, and internet communications, to withhold their votes from one or more directors in an effort to communicate a message of dissatisfaction.[3] The researchers found that boards do listen to such communications. After such a campaign, a CEO had a 25% probability of being dismissed within a year, 12.5 times the annual rate of 2% for CEOs in general.

For example, at the 2004 annual meeting of Walt Disney Co., shareholders initiated a "vote no" campaign against CEO Michael

Eisner and presiding director George Mitchell that resulted in 45% of votes being withheld from Eisner and 25% from Mitchell. Eisner resigned as board chair the following day.

The alliance between corporate managers and large institutions that manage clients' money—including investment banks and mutual funds—has also come under scrutiny.[4] By 2004, these institutional investors had to disclose how they voted in shareholder meetings and adopt policies ensuring that the votes were in their clients' interests.[5] Their actions were now public; the cost of not walking one's talk was higher. This has given more power to the voices of responsible investors. If they make a compelling point, their fellow shareholders, now forced to keep an eye open, might be inclined to join their protest.

As well as in the United States, the corporate governance trend is accelerating in Europe and other emerging markets. This evolution toward corporate democracy means that shareholders now get their turn to express their concerns and demand changes. They now have enough power that if they want to talk about social and environmental issues, managers have to listen.

▮▮▮▮▮ Shareholder Resolutions

In the United States, the mechanism through which investors "talk" is the process of the "shareholder resolution," a proposal submitted by stockholders for a vote at a company's annual meeting. A shareholder resolution to protest napalm manufacturer Dow Chemical resulted in a landmark 1970 U.S. court of appeals decision to prod the Securities and Exchange Commission (SEC) toward facilitating shareholder resolutions. The SEC requires that shareholders own at least $2,000 worth of shares in a company (or 1% of all shares) to file a shareholder proposal. In addition, they must own the stock for at least one year.

Shareholders submit resolutions dealing primarily with corporate governance, for example executive compensation, or corporate social responsibility issues, for example global warming, labor relations, tobacco smoking, and human rights. Typically, resolutions are opposed by the corporation's management, hence the insistence on a vote. Almost without exception, shareholder resolutions are defeated because they do not gain a majority of stockholder votes. According to SEC rules, defeated resolutions may be resubmitted only if they pass certain election hurdles (3% of votes must be affirmative in the first attempt; 6% in the second; and 10% in the third).

Despite losing in vote totals, shareholder activism has been influential. Resolutions are often effective at raising public awareness and thereby pressuring corporate management. Such pressure makes management willing to initiate a conversation with the shareholder who brings the proposal. If the management is willing to address the shareholder's concerns, the resolution is withdrawn.

Using internal data from TIAA-CREF, researchers Willard Carleton, James Nelson, and Michael Weisbach studied whether the giant asset manager was successful in getting companies to adopt changes. Their analysis, published in 1998, showed that more than 95% of the time when TIAA-CREF contacts a company to suggest changes, it eventually adopts them. The fund achieved this high success rate despite getting a majority vote in only one case.[6] Such is the arm-twisting power of a large fund!

Given these promising results, resolutions have been spearheaded by several coordinating groups. One such group active in social resolutions is the Interfaith Center on Corporate Responsibility, a coalition of 275 faith-based institutional investors and SRI firms with more than $100 billion in assets. Public pension funds and sovereign funds are also involved in submitting and supporting shareholder resolutions.

The participation of different investor groups in the shareholder resolutions process has caused an increase in the number of shareholder resolutions. In 2007, more than 1,150 shareholder resolutions were filed, and 331 of these were socially oriented. This represents a significant increase from the 220 socially oriented resolutions filed in 1999. Both environmental and social resolutions have increased. Of the 331 resolutions, some 80 were environmental proposals, and 43 dealt with climate change, compared with 31 in 2006.

As the number of such resolutions has kept increasing year after year, management has become more willing to discuss these issues. One-fourth of these environmental and social resolutions were withdrawn after management made significant concessions on these issues. In effect, such withdrawal achieves the shareholders' purpose and is equivalent to a majority vote.

Table 2.1 Impact of Social Shareholder Resolutions Filed by Calvert Funds.

Time period	Number of resolutions	Successfully withdrawn	Voted (average vote)	Unsuccessful	Success index
before 1990	3	2	0 (N.A.)	1	1
1991–1995	12	6	6 (15%)	0	3.9
1996–2000	15	8	6 (11.6%)	1	4.7
2001	14	10	3 (14.8%)	1	5.44
2002	24	16	6 (8.1%)	2	8.48
2003	17	8	9 (27.4%)	0	6.47
2004	32	15	11 (19%)	6	9.6
2005	22	16	1 (29%)	5	8.29
2006	17*	9	7 (29%)	0	6.06
2007	35**	20	20 (31.7%)	2	13.1

* One firm was acquired.
** One firm was acquired, and two firms hadn't yet voted at the time this table was published.

Source: Based on Calvert's data found at http:// www. calvert.com/sri_6979. html.

The resolutions that were put up for a vote also received more support than before. Climate change proposals won 20% of the vote, on average, in 2007; the average for environmental and social issues was 15%. These are both all-time highs for such proposals. Environmental advocacy groups such as the Coalition for Environmentally Responsible Economies and the Social Investment Forum are now preparing for bigger seasons ahead.

Here is an example of a resolution targeting Coca-Cola:

Proposal That Coca-Cola Company Report on Implementation of Beverage Container Recycling Strategy

WHEREAS Coca-Cola Company has repeatedly emphasized its commitment to environmental leadership. However, the majority of Coca-Cola beverage containers in the U.S. continues to be landfilled, incinerated or littered, thereby contributing to environmental pollution, and reducing the U.S. supply of recycled plastic.

Coca-Cola Company has made substantial progress toward its goal to incorporate 10% recycled content resin into its plastic beverage containers in North America by year-end 2005. In addition, Coca-Cola Company has joined with its beverage industry peers to form the Beverage Packaging Environmental Council (BPEC) in order to study declining beverage container recovery rates. However, Coca-Cola Company and BPEC have resisted adopting a publicly stated, quantitative goal to increase beverage container recovery rates.

We believe both recycled content and container recovery goals are essential to an effective recycling strategy.

Unfortunately, the U.S. recycling rates for beverage containers have declined significantly in recent years. The Container Recycling Institute (CRI) estimates that the recovery rate for PET [polyethylene terephthalate] plastic beverage containers declined from 37% in 1995 to 20% in

2004, the most recent year for which data is available. CRI also reports, based on data from the Aluminum Association and the U.S. Department of Commerce, that the aluminum can recycling rate fell from 65% in 1992 to 45% in 2004. Beverage container recycling rates of 70% and higher are being achieved in 11 U.S. states with container deposit legislation (or bottle bills). Significant container recovery rates are possible, as evidenced in these 11 states, and in countries like Norway and Sweden where companies have achieved beverage container recovery rates of more than 80%. On average, the U.S. states with beverage container deposit systems recover three times as many beverage containers as do states without deposits. Nevertheless, Coca-Cola and other members of the American Beverage Association actively oppose container deposit systems without putting forth a solution capable of achieving comparable recovery rates.

BE IT RESOLVED THAT Shareowners of Coca-Cola Company request that the board of directors review the efficacy of its container recycling program and prepare a report to shareholders, by September 1, 2006, on a recycling strategy that includes a publicly stated, quantitative goal for enhanced rates of beverage container recovery in the U.S. The report, to be prepared at reasonable cost, may omit confidential information.

SUPPORTING STATEMENT

We believe the requested report is in the best interest of Coca-Cola Company and its shareholders. Leadership in this area may protect the Coca-Cola brands and improve the company's reputation. We anticipate the report will detail the means and feasibility of achieving, as soon as practicable, a quantitative, beverage container recovery goal. The report should:

• include a cost-benefit analysis of the different container recovery options available, such as curbside and drop-off recycling, drop-off programs, container deposit systems, and voluntary company and industry programs;

- explain Coca-Cola Company's position on container deposit systems;
- and explain Coca-Cola's efforts to work with peers to establish industry-wide container recycling goals.

Such resolutions are being supported by more and more powerful shareholders.

Indeed, TIAA-CREF has explicitly stated that it intends to put its $437 billion assets under management at work to pursue responsibility issues: "We exercise our shareholder rights by seeking to influence the environmental, social and governance (ESG) policies of the companies in which we invest. We employ this strategy across TIAA-CREF's entire portfolio, not just in our socially screened offerings."[7]

In 2006, TIAA-CREF voted in favor of more than 43% of the corporate responsibility shareholder resolutions they could vote for in the United States (up from 19% in 2005). Even if they are not SRI investors themselves, large funds are likely to join forces with the votes of SRI investors when they believe their proposals could improve a company's value. For example, in 2006, large financial companies including J. P. Morgan, Morgan Stanley, E*Trade, Credit Suisse, and Schwab voted in favor of more than 20% of corporate responsibility shareholder resolutions.[8]

▮▮▮▮ **Financial Intermediation**

Intermediation drives the financial services industry. Shareholders like Sven hold shares in companies indirectly, through their holdings in mutual funds or pension funds. These intermediaries, who vote on behalf of their clients, provide a valuable service—that of aggregating values.

As more capital flows into funds that evaluate social and environmental factors, the voice of responsible investors grows louder. As a result, when people like Sven invest their dollars in an SRI fund, their voices reach corporate decision makers through their funds' membership in a group such as the Interfaith Council on Corporate Responsibility, boosting their efforts to file resolutions and engage with the management of various companies.

In addition, more institutions—even if they are not labeled as responsible investors—are paying attention to social and environmental concerns than before. The increase in the number of institutions that support the responsible movement has made SRI more powerful today than it was in the past.

Critics sometimes argue that the increase in SRI capital is overstated. As a fraction of total investment, the amount has remained close to one in ten dollars during the past 10 years. Both SRI funds and total funds have grown. But this ignores the fact that assets under supporting funds—not classified as SRI investors—have also grown dramatically.

Another example of this is Norway's sovereign fund, the Government Pension Fund, one of the largest funds, with over $350 billion in investments. In 2004, the Norway Ministry of Finance laid down ethical guidelines for this fund (as we discussed in chapter 1). In January 1, 2005, all voting in the equity portfolio was transferred to the central bank in order to achieve more concise and consistent voting in accordance with ethical principles. In 2006, the fund voted in favor of several social resolutions. These included:

1. That companies draw up ethical guidelines related to human rights and report on their compliance with these guidelines, particularly for operations in countries where human rights have traditionally not been respected

2. That companies report on sustainability and on the company's economic, social and environmental impact (triple-bottom-line accounting)

3. That companies report on their guidelines for equal rights for all employees and on the steps taken by the company to safeguard equal treatment

4. That companies in the petroleum sector report on the impact of their operations for the ecosystem in specific geographical areas

5. That companies in the petroleum sector report on how they will prepare for and adapt to regulatory changes related to climate change, and the effect this might have on their competitive situation

6. That companies publish or introduce guidelines based on internationally recognized standards concerning foreign suppliers working conditions, and that audits of these conditions are carried out and reports submitted

This is just one example among the 100 institutional investors who globally represent $11 trillion in assets and have signed the Principles for Responsible Investment. Institutional shareholders who invest on behalf of investors like Sven now have a loudspeaker. As a result, when they speak about the values Sven expects them to address, their words will be heard by corporate decision makers.

At the launch of the Principles for Responsible Investment at the New York Stock Exchange on April 27, 2006, UN Secretary-General Kofi A. Annan said: "They offer a path for integrating environmental, social and governance criteria into investment analysis and ownership practices. If implemented, they have tremendous potential to more closely align investment practices with the goals of the United Nations, thereby contributing to a more stable and inclusive global economy."

▪▪▪▪   **From the Ear to the Hand**

Sven left his meeting with Tim still skeptical. He no longer doubted the power of his voice and its ability—in concert with other socially responsible investors—to be heard by companies worldwide. Still, he wondered whether reaching the corporate ear was enough to move the corporate hand into action. Listening does not mean that management will respond. Sven knew that these resolutions rarely win. Further, even if they do, shareholder resolutions are not binding. Managers don't have to follow them.

Sven wanted to know: Are management concessions and willingness to work with socially concerned shareholders isolated examples? If not, what drives management to make these changes? Are their responses mere lip service? At that point, Tim had opinions but no concrete answers for Sven. He promised to explore these matters further. Sven's interest was also piqued. He wanted to know what Tim would find. As Tim looked into the reasons companies might be compelled to respond in a meaningful manner to socially responsible investors, he discovered a few key factors.

▪▪▪▪   **Investors Affect Stock Prices**

The most common argument advocates of SRI present is based on two premises:

1. As a responsible investor, you can affect stock prices.
2. Managers care about stock prices.

Consequently, managers will respond to socially responsible investors. If they threaten to sell their stock because the company is violating human rights, the management will take steps to appease them. Conversely, if investors reward firms that act in socially responsible ways with a higher stock price, then the firm is more likely to continue doing so.

Few question the second premise. A large part of executive compensation is directly tied to the performance of corporate stock. Stock prices also indirectly provide managers with benefits such as the ability to use stock to acquire smaller companies. But few from the non-SRI camp truly believe that responsible investors affect prices.

A criticism that has been made constantly over the years is that such investors are not large enough in number to affect stock prices. The amount of assets under SRI, however, has been constantly growing. Today, $2.1 trillion in the United States—or $1 of every $10—are invested by socially responsible investors. Over the next three to five years, this number should double.

That there aren't enough responsible investors is therefore a fading criticism. The stronger criticism is that not all responsible investors agree on what is responsible. As a result, even though $2.1 trillion dollars are at work for socially responsible causes, the amount per cause might be much smaller and possibly negligible.

If these funds agree on common values, there is no reason why they cannot impact stock prices.

A study by Robert Heinkel, Alan Kraus, and Josef Zechner (at the University of British Columbia and the University of Vienna) derives the impact of values-based investors on stock prices in a theoretical model of the stock market.[9] The study shows that managers who maximize the value of their firm might choose to spend on social responsibility even if it has a negative impact on business profits—in order to attract values-based investors. The reason is that by having access to more investors, responsible firms have a lower cost of capital, which increases a firm's value and can more than offset the spending required to comply with responsible investors' criteria. The study also shows that the stock prices of "bad" firms can be significantly discounted even if only 10% of the investors are values-based.

This theoretical exercise has also found support in real-world prices. Most funds that manage SRI screen out tobacco stocks; this is one "value" that many funds—rightly or not—currently agree on. So if these investors had any effect at all, we should find it in the tobacco industry. A research study has shown just that: stock prices of tobacco firms trade at a discount to comparable firms in other sectors.[10] This discount was estimated to be 15%. Such a discount did not exist before the advent of socially responsible funds or when social norms toward tobacco were more accommodating.

Several SRI funds use membership in socially responsible indices (such as the FTSE4good) to identify which companies are leaders in responsible decision making. If SRI assets are large enough to affect stock prices (if only temporarily), one would expect companies that exit such a major responsible index to experience a drop in their stock prices. It is indeed the case. In a recent working paper of the Federal Reserve Bank of Atlanta, researchers Leonardo Becchetti, Rocco Ciciretti, and Iftekhar Hasan showed that when an exit from the Domini 400 Social Index (one of the major social indices in the U.S.) is announced, the exiting company experiences significant abnormal returns.[11] The study looks at all involuntary exits from the index between 1990 and 2004; the stock price drop is about 3%. Certainly enough for managers to care.

Together, these studies show that even at current levels, the amount of capital dedicated to SRI can impact prices. Consequently, companies' managers and investor relations offices are likely to respond to responsible investors and their concerns.

Maintaining Loyalty

Not all money is the same. Terms such as *smart money* and *dumb money* are now commonplace in financial jargon. In some ways, capital has personality, too. Take another personality trait—loyalty. Some shareholders are short term oriented, as is their money. Short-term trading often drives short-term prices. This has led many to believe that investor sentiment is an important determinant of short-term prices. Several prominent investors share this view as well. As Warren Buffett, a legendary investor, has summed it up, "in the short term the market is a popularity contest; in the long term it is a weighing machine." In the same context, he once stated: "Indeed, we believe that according the name 'investors' to institutions that trade actively is like calling someone who repeatedly engages in one-night stands a romantic."

Many corporate executives do not want to partner with such institutions. Many managers have voiced concerns about the tension between satisfying short-term investors and taking decisions to maximize business value. Academic researchers have found that indeed corporate investment decisions cater to investor sentiment.[12] Professors Natasha Burns, Simi Kedia and Marc Lipson (of the University of Texas at San Antonio, Rutgers University, and the University of Virginia, respectively) have shown that the presence of short term–oriented investors increases managerial incentives to manage earnings.[13] In addition, in a 2003 study, Edith Hotchkiss and Deon Strickland (of Boston College and Arizona State University) found that when firms report lower-than-forecasted earnings, the stock price response to the announcement is significantly more negative for firms with a higher proportion of short-term investors.[14] Little wonder, then, that ambitious managers who wish to pursue long-term goals want to attract and retain long-term investors: In case things do not run perfectly smoothly, the company will be less exposed to excessively negative reactions of the stock price.

Google is a prominent and recent illustration of managers' preference for long-term investors. When the company went public, its founders wrote:

> Many companies are under pressure to keep their earnings in line with analysts' forecasts. Therefore, they often accept smaller, predictable earnings rather than larger and less predictable returns. Sergey and I feel this is harmful, and we intend to steer in the opposite direction....
>
> Google has had adequate cash to fund our business and has generated additional cash through operations. This gives us the flexibility to weather costs, benefit from opportunities and optimize our long term earnings. For example, in our ads system we make many improvements that affect revenue in both directions. These are in areas like end user relevance and satisfaction, advertiser satisfaction, partner needs and targeting technology. We release improvements immediately rather than delaying them, even though delay might give "smoother" financial results. You have our commitment to execute quickly to achieve long term value rather than making the quarters more predictable.
>
> Our long term focus does have risks. Markets may have trouble evaluating long term value, thus potentially reducing the value of our company. Our long term focus may simply be the wrong business strategy. Competitors may be rewarded for short term tactics and grow stronger as a result. As potential investors, you should consider the risks around our long term focus.[15]

As this letter and Buffett suggest, catering to short-term investors through business decisions impairs business value.

> Did you know that a $10,000 investment in Berkshire Hathaway in 1965, the year Warren Buffett took control of it, would grow to be worth nearly $45 million by October 2007? By comparison, $10,000 in the S & P 500 would have grown to only about $600,000. Whether you like him or not, Buffett's investment strategy is arguably one of the most successful ever.

But takeovers highlight a concern some shareholders have about managerial preference for long-term investors. It has been shown that takeovers are more likely when investors are short term oriented.[16] While shareholder value might increase with takeovers, typically, managers like to acquire and not be acquired. Thus managers' preference for long-term investors might also reflect a desire to preserve their own jobs and enjoy a "quiet life." What drives managers to seek long-term investors is thus open to debate. But what is clear is that managers such as Larry Page and Sergey Brin can find an ally in responsible investors.

Responsible investors are often long-term investors.

Why are socially responsible investors long term oriented? Many, for example pension funds, invest on behalf of investors who have long horizons. These funds do not face the threat of monthly or quarterly withdrawals as many mutual and hedge funds do. This might reflect the loyalty of their clients, who are not purely driven by performance but also by values. A look at flows to the mutual fund sector between 1999 and 2001—a period marked by a stock market crash—shows the relative loyalty of socially responsible investors. While the amount of new assets going to all mutual funds dropped by 94%, there was only a 54% decline in new assets destined for SRI funds.[17] In a recent study, Professor Nicolas Bollen from Vanderbilt University found that flows in and out of socially responsible funds are significantly less volatile than for other funds.[18] He also found that investors in socially responsible funds are less prone to pull out assets after negative returns than investors in conventional funds and concludes that "Mutual fund companies…can expect socially responsible investors to be more loyal than in ordinary funds."

Many who seek to engage in a dialogue with corporate managers to address their environmental and social concerns believe that they are more likely to have an impact as shareholders. Consequently, they continue to hold on to shares as long as possible. The SEC requires stock owners who wish to file a shareholder resolution to have held their shares for at least a year. For such a fund, selling its shares is the last resort—a final call to action.

Responsible investors thus belong to the category of Buffett-like investors who are less likely to jump ship simply because the share price is falling on a given day. This ability to withstand downturns and using convictions to allay anxiety is what makes many responsible investors long term oriented.

▪▮▮▪▪   **Managing Risk**

Managers in corporate headquarters are also likely to keep a finger on the pulse of SRI for business reasons. Often, actions on the part of a responsible investor provide support to less powerful groups that have been targeting corporations. Consider, for example, the case of Home Depot. A consumer boycott organized by rainforest-related nongovernmental organizations was given a strong impetus when shareholders joined the protest. Socially conscious investors combine with other groups such as consumers, employees, and nonprofit organizations to forge a powerful voice.

Investors are viewed as more moderate in their views and relatively mainstream compared to radical or liberal groups that target corporations. If investors join hands with a group viewed as extreme, this provides a powerful endorsement of the group's cause. Such mainstreaming of the views of smaller groups forces everyone to pay greater attention to the group's concerns. As more people—employees and customers included—focus on the issue the group is highlighting, the risk increases that the corporation's business will be disrupted. Corporate managers thus have every reason to keep an eye on shareholder concerns and they tend to act fast when such issues first arise.

One large U.S. corporation that has been accused of irresponsible behavior is Wal-Mart. The Council of Ethics, which was founded in 2004, in its recommendation to the Norwegian Pension Fund of November 15, 2005, said:

> An extensive body of material indicates that Wal-Mart consistently and systematically employs minors in contravention of international rules, that working conditions at many of its suppliers are dangerous or health-hazardous, that workers are pressured into working overtime without compensation, that the company systematically discriminates against women in pay, that all attempts to unionize by the company's employees are stopped, that employees are in a number of cases unreasonably punished and locked in, along with a number of other circumstances.... What makes this case special is the sum total of ethical norm violations, both in the company's own business operations and in the supplier chain. It appears to be a systematic and planned practice on the part of the company to hover at, or cross, the bounds of what are accepted norms for the work environment.... Many of the violations are serious, most appear to be systematic, and altogether they form a picture of a company whose overall activity displays a lack of willingness to countervail violations of norms in its business operations.[19]

Wal-mart had not responded to the Council's letter dated September 14, 2005. Finally, in June 2006, the Norwegian fund sold its shares in Wal-mart. Wal-mart has since taken steps to strengthen its commitment to social responsibility. During fiscal year 2006 (February 1, 2006—January 31, 2007), Wal-mart initiated the following steps. The audit schedule for factories rated "low-risk violations" increased from one year to two years. Unannounced audits increased to 26% of total audits. Auditors began to use tablet PCs to enter violations and produce the onsite report during an audit. The International Giving Program, focusing on giving back to the communities where merchandise for Wal-Mart is sourced and sold, awarded its first grant to the Asia Foundation to fund scholarships for migrant women in China. Wal-mart's *Ethical Standards*' audit scope expanded to include audits of certain factories producing domestically sourced merchandise. The sample for worker interviews and documentation review increased from 15 to 25 workers, which is industry best practice.

A higher amount of SRI capital for a cause also strengthens the lobbying efforts for that cause. In some cases, the SRI fund directly attempts to lobby for changes in regulation. In 2007, 30 leading investors who collectively manage more than $1.4 trillion in assets sent a letter to the U.S. Congress advocating the passage of a national energy bill for the expansion of clean energy, reduction of oil dependence, and curbing of pollution that causes global warming.[20] Since a firm's business prospects are related to its awareness of the dynamic regulatory landscape, paying attention to SRI capital and investors might mitigate any such regulatory risk.

Tim found out that SRI works as we have described here. He summarized these findings and sent them to both Kathy and to Sven. To Sven, he wrote:

With regard to our conversation about socially responsible investing, please find attached some examples of what corporations have done. I will be curious to hear from you which of these actions you would consider lip service and which would motivate you to allocate some of your money to socially responsible funds.

- Coke agreed to invest $60 million to build the world's largest plastic bottle recycling plant in South Carolina. It also committed to recycle or reuse 100% of PET plastic used by the company's beverages in U.S. sales. The company spent $16 million this year to promote recycling through its own recycling division, as well as by investing $2 million in RecycleBank, a new startup that promotes incentive-based curbside recycling.
- Apache and Anadarko, two oil companies in the United States, agreed to report their responses to climate change.
- Wendy's International, a fast food chain, has decided to produce a report on its social and environmental performance.
- Target Inc/ has agreed to publish its first sustainability report.
- Talisman, a Canadian oil company, has divested its business that supplied oil to the Sudanese government due to the "Sudan discount" in its share price.
- Baxter International, a maker of health-care products, agreed to stop using polyvinyl chloride (PVC), which releases carcinogens when it is burned, in some of its products.
- McDonald's and Disney are investing considerable effort and resources in monitoring the labor conditions under which Disney products for sale at McDonald's branches are made.
- Procter & Gamble began to sell Fair Trade Certified coffee after an intensive dialogue with socially responsible

investors. The Fair Trade certification system helps to alleviate poverty and hardship by guaranteeing farmers a minimum price per pound for their crop, and by supporting democratically managed cooperatives and more environmentally sound farming techniques.

- Gap Inc. released its first Social Responsibility Report after two years of dialogue with Domini and other socially responsible investors. Gap became the first clothing retailer to publicly rate the way its contractors treat their workers, and set new standards of transparency for its industry.

The Coca-Cola example shows the power of shareholder resolutions. Sandy Douglas, president of Coca-Cola North America, acknowledged in a press conference that its commitments were partly the result of engagement by social investments groups. The Gap example brings us back to the news story that first set in motion Kathy's curiosity. That story didn't end there. Thanks to prior dialogues with socially responsible investors, executives at the Gap had already started paying attention to such social matters before the sweatshop story broke. So they were prepared; soon after the news stories appeared, they immediately pulled the product in question from the shelves and called a meeting with all their suppliers to ensure that such incidents were not repeated. Clearly, the Gap recognized that its brand was highly vulnerable to charges of corporate irresponsibility. In a response to the incident to India's NDTV, Dr. Raymond Fisman, Professor of Social Enterprise, Columbia Business School, said that the shift from "the 'Nike response' in the mid-1990s to the Gap's recent actions…gives…a sense of how things have changed. In some ways it probably [has been]…cases like Nike that [have]…brought about such a change because it has made companies realize exactly how vulnerable they are." And perhaps it wasn't simply a reputation cost that GAP was trying to minimize. A group of US senators, including Hilary Clinton and Barak Obama, are pushing for legislation at U.S. Senate Commerce Subcommittee hearings that calls for a ban on importing any products made in sweatshops. If such a law becomes reality, companies that have anticipated the coming changes and acted on them will be better positioned to do business in the new environment.

To conclude, corporations are increasingly likely to listen and to act on the concerns of responsible investors. While some of these reactions might be lip service (which of Tim's examples do you think are mere lip service?), they are also becoming more meaningful.

3

Profits or Values?

 **Concerns about Diversification**

"Are you sure?" asked Anthony, a professional financial advisor hired by a young firm to advise its employees on their pension allocations. The firm had grown rapidly and was well on their way to an initial public offering in the stock market. In anticipation of this watershed event, the firm had set up a pension plan. With Anthony's help, the employees were to decide where to invest. As he usually did, Anthony used the meeting to gauge risk characteristics of different employees. He asked them about how they saw themselves living in five years, and in 15 years. Did they have kids to care for, did they have any loans? He asked if they had any loans. It was a standard list of questions—he didn't have to look at the list any more. He was taken by surprise when Guy walked into the room and said directly that he wanted to invest all his money in socially responsible funds.

Guy had worked in the corporate world for 15 years—for a firm that millions of people around the world know. In search of a nimbler, smaller venture, where he could create something new, he had joined the start-up. He knew of SRI because his previous employer was one of the increasing number of firms that give employees the option of investing their 401 K money in SRI funds.

A 2007 study showed that 1 in 5 401(k) plans provide employees with this option. Even more striking, half the plans that currently did not offer an SRI option were planning to do so in the next three years.[1] This means that by 2010, three out of five defined contribution plans will provide employees with a socially responsible option. According to the study, 81% of plan administrators, 72% of consultants, and 47% of plan sponsors predict an increasing or steady demand for SRI over the next five years.

The major forces behind this trend include a desire to align retirement plan offerings with the employer's mission (e.g., a focus on corporate social responsibility); internal staff recommendations; and employee-participant requests. And several corporate executives have expressed enthusiasm. For example, Dave Stangis, director of corporate responsibility at Intel, has said: "As a company continually striving to lead in socially responsible business practices, it just made good business sense to have an option that allowed our employees to put their money where their hearts are. Our employees are diverse and have strong views on why it's important for the company they work for to be socially responsible. Part of meeting that expectation, now and in the future, means having 401K investment choices that are broad and include SRI options."[2]

Measuring Financial Performance: The Risk-Return Trade-Off

The characteristics of a financial product can be represented by two main dimensions—"expected returns" and "risk." The "expected returns" are the average profits one can anticipate if one invests in the product; "risk" indicates how uncertain these profits are. A financial product is considered "efficient" if no product provides higher expected returns for the same level of risk. Incorporating SRI in one's portfolio—like any other constraint—can have two types of costs: a lower level of expected returns or a higher level of risk.

▨▨▨▨▨ The Power of Diversification

Due to this increasing interest in SRI, Anthony knew about SRI funds. He was aware of SRI's growth and was still becoming familiar with its risk and return characteristics. There were a lot of recent findings—a large pile of research and policy papers. Since he had not yet taken the time to go through them rigorously, his classical finance training determined his view. He thought that SRI would come at a financial cost because it meant giving up some of the benefit of diversification.

Why is the lack of diversification costly? Imagine we are playing a game. We "flip a coin," and you bet a dollar on the outcome. Heads, you win three times your initial stake ($3); tails, you lose the dollar ($0).

Let's say you invest in that game all the money you have in your wallet, say $30. The probability that you lose all of it is 50%. If you win, you get $90 (3 × $30). Since the chances of getting a heads or a tails outcome are equal, the chances of winning are 50% or 0.5. This means that after the game, on an average, you end up with (0.5 × 90 + 0.5 × 0) = $45.

Now, imagine that you instead play this game 30 times, betting $1.00 each time. Each time there is a 50% chance that you win $3.00. On average, you end up with $1.50. If you played this 30 times, the average amount you could expect would be $45 (30 × $1.50). So, as before, you can again expect to end up with $45. However, the risk in this second game is much smaller.

The likelihood that you will end up with an empty wallet in the first game is 50%. This will happen when you are wrong. But in the second game, the probability that you end up with an empty wallet is a number that is smaller than 0.000000001. In fact, the probability that you end up with less than $30 is now only about 2%. As you can see, splitting your bet into smaller independent ones has a tremendous impact on the level of risk you are taking: The risk of ending up with less than what you initially had in your wallet falls from 50% to 2% by splitting your bet into 30 small independent bets.

This intuition carries over directly to stock investing. Having a diversified portfolio, as opposed to selecting a few stocks, will make your returns much less risky.

Screening

Anthony was familiar with these statistical phenomena, which mathematicians call "the law of large numbers." In his view, lower diversification was a consequence, hence a drawback, of SRI. He based this conclusion on one simple fact: *Most SRI funds use negative screens to exclude entire sectors.* "Screening" is the application of a criterion to either select or remove companies in the investment process; the former is often referred to as *positive* screening, the latter as *negative* or *exclusionary* screening.

All investors apply screens to their investments. An investor might choose to "invest in stocks with a low price-to-earnings ratio." This is an example of a *financial* screen. A *social* screen is a nonfinancial criterion that relates to the way a company operates or the characteristics of its products. In general, screening divides companies into those the investor considers suitable and not suitable—for social or financial reasons or a combination of both.

Social screening remains controversial 37 years after Pax launched the first SRI mutual fund, and generations after Quakers and evangelicals began the practice. Because they considered drinking and smoking sinful, these early investors eliminated alcohol and tobacco companies from their portfolios. This industry-based negative screening did not take any financial characteristics into account. Consequently, many critics of this procedure have focused on the loss in financial performance.

If "sin industries" formed a large fraction of the economy, removing them from one's portfolio would create significant disadvantages, in that the resulting portfolio would be more risky because it had fewer stocks. In financial markets—as in many other activities—not all risk is rewarded. Risk that gets a commensurate reward is called "systematic risk," and the risk without a reward is termed "idiosyncratic risk." Removing entire industries often increases the bad kind of risk—the idiosyncratic—leaving one with more risk but no proportional reward. For this reason, critics of SRI contend, removing companies involved in entire sectors must involve a financial cost.

Why Screening Out an Entire Industry Is Costly in Terms of Risk

In 1990, Bill Sharpe and Harry Markowitz received the Nobel Prize in economics for their work on modern portfolio theory.[3] A key insight of their research was that investors get rewarded for "systematic" risk—risk that affects many companies—and not for "idiosyncratic" risk—risk that is unique to a company. One can build an efficient portfolio by diversifying—that is, by averaging the idiosyncratic risk over several firms.

(continued)

Let's say you are invested in a homebuilding firm. Which firm would provide your portfolio with better offsetting diversification—another firm in the homebuilding industry or a firm from another industry, say health care? Or are the two equally powerful in cancelling idiosyncratic risk?

Companies in an industry tend to move together, as they are affected by the same type of macroeconomic news. For example, positive news about home sales lifts all homebuilders, and negative new brings them all down. So a firm from the health-care sector—a sector largely unrelated to homebuilding—would provide a significant diversifying benefit.

Avoiding an entire industry from which one could select one's diversifying stock will have a greater cost than avoiding other industry peers. In the example, avoiding health-care companies entirely would be more costly than avoiding other homebuilders.

Anthony subscribed to this view. Most SRI options he was familiar with had a rule to not invest in companies making profits from tobacco, alcohol, gaming, and weapons. For SRI advocates, avoiding these 'sin' industries was the investor's equivalent of a punishment. For Anthony, this meant that there would be a cost to stick to SRI.

One might think that this argument would hold only if we excluded large industries. In other words, removing large industries such as the oil industry would have a high cost of diversification, but removing small sectors should not have a significant impact. After all, companies involved in tobacco, alcohol, and gambling nowadays account for less than 10% of the S & P 500 market capitalization. And these are usually the industries that SRI funds remove.

However, screening smaller sectors such as tobacco and alcohol is not innocuous. That's because these "sin industries" have some financially attractive features. For example, companies that sell tobacco or alcohol tend to have a stable (or addicted) customer base, making their profits less prone to wild gyrations. Consequently, they are a useful addition to a portfolio, as they stabilize returns throughout downturns and poor economic periods. The stocks of firms in sectors such as alcohol and tobacco are less sensitive to market downturns. The *beta*, a commonly used indicator of how much a stock or an industry index follows the behavior of the entire equity market, measures the change in stock performance for a 1% change in the overall market performance. While beta is 1.4 for the semiconductor industry and 1.2 for computers, it is only 0.74 for tobacco and 0.76 for alcohol. That means these sectors fall less when the broad market falls. In a defensive portfolio, braced for an upcoming downturn, these stocks therefore add value and usually outperform less "sinful" ones. On Wall Street, there is an apt saying: "When the going gets tough, the tough get drinking, smoking, and gambling."

A recent study by Harrison Hong at Princeton University and Marcin Kacperczyk at the University of British Columbia showed that "sin" stocks outperformed a comparable set of "less sinful" stocks by approximately 5% a year.[4] This outperformance was higher during times when the entire equity market was falling. For example, since the beginning of 2000, during months in which the S & P 500 fell by more than 2%, sin stocks have outperformed the S & P 500 by an average of 3.5% per month! On the other hand, this outperformance is reduced to an average of 1.5% per month during months in which the S & P 500 has gained more than 2%.

Since the contribution of sin stocks is roughly 10% of the broad market, this means that a portfolio excluding sin stocks would yield on average (over a long period such as 10 years) 0.5% less a year than the market. Of course, if one were to expand the definition of sin stocks, more firms would be excluded, and the lack-of-diversification cost could increase substantially.

To summarize: What happens if you exclude sin stocks from your portfolio? Long-term investors who typically invest in the S & P 500 are likely to face a small cost—an average cost of 0.50% on a yearly basis. This cost will be higher during downturns. Consider the example of The California State Teachers' Retirement System, which dumped its tobacco holdings in 2000, just before a major market downturn. A report presented to the board estimated that the cost of the tobacco ban for the retirement fund between 2001 and 2007 was more than $1 billion.[5]

During good times, this cost will vanish and might even translate into profits. Several studies that show SRI funds have outperformed non-SRI funds often use these good times to conduct their study. Depending on the period one chooses and on how many years of recessions it contains, one can find sensibly different answers to the question whether SRI funds overperform or underperform. While there is no consensus on the relative performance of SRI funds compared to non-SRI funds, most academic studies find only small differences. Christopher Geczy, Robert Stambaugh, and David Levin, of the Wharton School of the University of Pennsylvania, found in 2005 that, due to lack of diversification, restricting one's investment to SRI mutual funds costs a few basis points (1 basis point = 0.01% = 0.0001) a month.[6] Sally Hamilton, Hoje Jo, and Meir Statman analyzed the returns of socially screened mutual funds (1993) and found that they are statistically indistinguishable from those of unscreened funds.[7]

A recent survey, conducted by Greenberg Quinlan Rosner Research (based in Washington, D.C.), canvassed 1,002 TIAA-CREF participants, of whom half invest in the CREF Social Choice Account and half do not. Majorities of both sets of

respondents showed a willingness to accept lower returns if
their investments could "do some good in this world," with 81%
of SCA participants agreeing and 64% non-SCA participants
supporting this.

So, given what Anthony knew about SRI, his response to Guy's
request was skeptical: "On the basis of studies I have seen, I
think excluding sin stocks from your equity market portfolio
will cost you around 0.50% to 1% a year. Let us break this down.
If you invest $10,000 for 15 years, you would lose approximately
$1,500. Do you really want to do this?" He continued, "If you
allocated 30% of your portfolio to SRI products but used the
remaining for traditional products, the cost would be only $300
over 15 years. That is around $20 a year." He added, emphatically:
"But the choice is yours. How much does expressing your values
in your portfolio matter to you? How much are you willing to
pay?" For Guy, the answer was simple. There were no trade-
offs. He would simply not feel good if he invested in tobacco or
alcohol. It was against his faith. It was not a matter of returns.
Nonetheless, for many others who met with Anthony that day
to discuss their portfolios, this was a difficult question.

"TIAA-CREF believes that investors do not have to give up
returns to invest in a screened universe," said Amy O'Brien,
who was installed as director of social investing at TIAA-CREF
in June 2005. "The CREF Social Choice Account is an SRI
option that offers competitive returns." A balanced fund, the
SCA has closely tracked its benchmark, a weighted composite
of the Russell 3000 (60%) for stocks and the Lehman Brothers
U.S. Aggregate Index (40%) for bonds. "The CREF Social
Choice Account is an SRI option that offers competitive
returns."

The "Industry-Agnostic" Approach: The Recipe

Is this Faustian choice, between values and profits, inevitable? Actually, it's not. An investor practicing SRI can opt for an option less drastic than avoiding broad industries: excluding within each industry the least responsible companies. Many responsible funds often call this the "best-in-class" approach. The resulting portfolio will still have companies in industries such as tobacco.

A fund manager trying to construct such an industry-agnostic responsible portfolio for her customers has to decide how much to invest in each company in a manner that reflects the concerns both financial performance and for responsibility. How does she proceed? Here is a recipe.

Step 1: Collect information on responsibility. The fund manager needs to know the characteristics of her "ingredients" or to find information on companies social and environmental responsibility. This information is available from research companies that specialize in these issues, for example, KLD Analytics, one of the U.S. leaders in social responsibility information. This company reviews more than three thousand U.S. corporations, including every company on the S & P 500. After analyzing public sources of information, KLD produces a score for each company that indicates the level of its "strengths" and its "concerns" in regard to each issue, for example, community, diversity, employee relations, human rights, product safety, pollution, and climate change. Using KLD scores, the fund manager can rank companies in every industry in the order of their social responsibility scores.

Step 2: Remove companies that do not pass the bar. The fund manager now "picks ingredients." Using the data from KLD, she eliminates, for each year, the companies that show a lack of responsibility. To be specific, starting in 1999, she keeps the firms that belong to the S & P 500 index and for which KLD reports (that year) *no concerns* in any of three areas—environment, customers (product safety), and employee treatment.[8] That leaves her with about 150 firms a year. This is a selective responsibility screen, since she has "failed" three out of five companies in the S & P 500. Her portfolio, however, includes hotel companies, for example Marriott or Wyndham, that own casinos. Even though they generate only a minor fraction of their profits from "sin industries," all these companies would be removed if one used traditional industry-based screening.

Step 3: Getting the right mix of industries. The fund manager now needs to decide how much to invest in each company. In her selection, she has eliminated more firms in some industries than others. For example, she has selected 9 of the 15 computer companies of the S & P 500, and only four of the 24 oil companies.

In cooking, the proportions of ingredients matter. Having a lot of bacon and only two eggs in your refrigerator does not imply that you should put more bacon in your omelet! When constructing a finance portfolio, the same rationale applies. The fund manager wants to preserve a high diversification across industries, which is financially attractive as it limits risk. In her recipe, she will invest in each industry to the same proportion that it is represented in the S & P 500. This means that if an industry has relatively few responsible companies, she will invest relatively more in these companies. For example, she will invest large amounts in the two oil companies we have selected to compensate for the fact that most of the oil companies have been thrown out.

> The Capital Asset Pricing Model (CAPM), a widely used theory developed by Nobel prize–winner William Sharpe, provides some guidance on what portion of one's investment money one should allocate to a given industry when trying to form an efficient portfolio. According to the theory, the money allocated to a given industry should reflect the portion of the market that the industry represents, as measured by the market capitalization of firms.

The fund manager has now finished constructing her responsible portfolio. It retains the same properties of industry diversification as the S & P 500. Relative to the S & P 500, the portfolio does not overinvest or underinvest in any industry. Consequently, the responsible portfolio is not exposed to any directional moves in sectors relative to the S & P 500 index.

▊▊▊▊▊ **Testing the Recipe**

To "taste" the recipe and find out if it expresses her preferences for social responsibility while avoiding any additional financial risk, the fund manager could do some "backtesting"—looking at how the recipe would have performed in the past. Figure 3.1 shows the monthly returns—the percentage by which a portfolio would change each month—of her responsible portfolio versus the S & P 500 from January 1999 until the end of 2007.

As you can see, the two portfolios are *strikingly similar*, to the point where they are difficult to distinguish visually. In 80% of the months, the difference in returns between both is less than 1.5%. Over this period, the responsible portfolio actually has an average monthly return (.52%) superior to the S & P 500 (.40%). The level of risk is slightly higher: The monthly "volatility"—the measure of how shaky returns are—is 3.9% for the S & P 500 and 4.2% for the responsible portfolio. Looking at

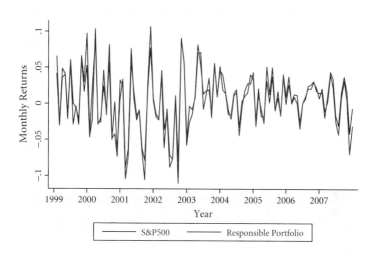

Figure 3.1 Industry-balanced Responsible Portfolio vs. S & P 500 (Monthly Returns).

losses, there are 10 months out of 108 for which the responsible portfolio has a return inferior to −5% and 11 months for which the S & P 500 returns less than −5%. Using that metric of risk, which measures the probability of strongly negative performance, the two portfolios appear similar.

To get a clearer picture of the comparative performance of both portfolios, another way to look at the data is to consider "cumulative returns," which means computing for each month the percentage by which the portfolio would have grown since 1999 (see fig. 3.2).

This graph shows that $100 invested in the S & P 500 in 1999 would have yielded $135 at the end of 2007, while the same amount invested in the responsible portfolio would have yielded $150. What is noticeable in this graph is that during the downturn of 2001–2003, the responsible portfolio does not behave worse than the S & P 500. Indeed, when the market

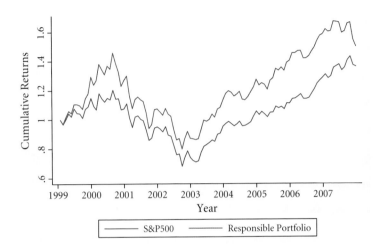

Figure 3.2 Industry-balanced Responsible Portfolio vs. S & P 500 (Cumulative Returns).

falls by 1%, the responsible portfolio does not tend to fall by more than 1%.[9] All in all, the responsible portfolio has slightly superior average returns and only marginally more risk, despite having 70% fewer stocks.

This example shows that an industry-agnostic selection method can be used to construct a portfolio that expresses strong responsibility preferences without giving up returns or significantly raising risk. For every industry, companies will remain after an industry-agnostic screening. Because they have the "flavor" of their industry in terms of risks and returns, they can be used to "represent" it in a portfolio. Preserving industry balance in this way is "risk-preserving," as opposed to an approach that excludes entire industries. Marc J. Lane, who runs a Chicago-based investment firm, has published a monograph documenting the success of this approach, and he argues that SRI ought to move toward using it instead of avoiding entire industries.[10] After studying the returns of the best-in-class companies from January 1995 to December 2003, he concludes that this approach "can empower investors—without eliminating entire industries—to deploy capital in a way that gives voice to their values and principles." He adds: "This expression of values can be accomplished without sacrificing either diversification or long-term performance."

This message is particularly relevant for investors who are not willing to pay a cost for being socially responsible. They would be interested in SRI if they knew they could do so without hurting their portfolio's performance.

████ The Recipe Catches On

Long after Guy left and Anthony finished his assignment with the start-up, he asked himself if all this wasn't just theory. The answer is no; for a movement is actually taking place in this direction, inspired by verifiable results. Companies providing responsibility indices and SRI asset managers have been taking into account an increased demand for balanced industry composition. The decision made by Pax World in 2006 to drop its zero tolerance policy on alcohol and gambling after it was forced by that policy to divest Starbucks is emblematic of this evolution. (Pax World still excludes tobacco and weapons.)

Dow Jones Sustainability Indexes and Sustainable Asset Management announced in 2002 that they would stop excluding companies from their responsible indexes simply because they operate in a so-called sin sector such as arms or tobacco. According to Sustainable Asset Management managing director Alexander Barkawi, "We cater to mainstream investors who want to be exposed to the entire economy in their portfolios."

In November 2006, KLD Research & Analytics launched its Global Sustainability Index, which uses the best-in-class methodology, and Northern Trust will distribute a mutual fund based on this index. Unlike KLD's previous indices—which include Domini, the poster child of SRI—this index does not exclude industries outright but selects stocks on the basis of their environmental, social, and governance performances. On the basis of KLD's ranking, the more responsible half of each industry is selected. For instance, an alcohol maker that makes sure its marketing aimed at young people is responsible might now be included. Due to adjustments such as these, this new index includes many firms that had previously been removed due to their line of business. As a result, the index contains some classic "sin" stocks, including hotel operators Accor SA, Marriott International, and Hilton Hotels (which also runs casinos) and retailers Woolworths and Coles Group (which sells liquor). "There is a re-examination of these issues, how to apply the screens and ultimately their purposes," says Thomas Kuh, managing director for KLD Indexes. "It represents the evolution and the maturing of the market."

Moral Issues: Promoting Change versus Zero Tolerance

When Anthony left, he realized he had asked Guy the wrong question. Perhaps no Faustian choice between values and profits was necessary after all. But beyond the financial issue there was another tricky question—a moral one.

Just as SRI has developed since Pax World started its first screened fund over seven decades ago, social screens have evolved beyond simple industry exclusions, though they remain prevalent. They are still important for some values-based investors like Guy. The expression of their values does not straddle black and white but falls on one side or the other. For Guy, tobacco companies are immoral. How much damage control they do or how much of their profits they give away does not influence his decision. Simple industry exclusions avoid any moral dilemma that investors like Guy might have to face.

While providing individual satisfaction and moral clarity for such faith-based investors, such divestment, it must be kept in mind, is not likely to have a direct effect on corporate behavior. Tobacco, alcohol, and gambling companies are unlikely to change their lines of business because of investor divestment. They are "stuck." The cost they would have to incur to attract responsible investors is too high: They would simply have to give up on most of their current activities.

So Guy, by refusing to invest in industries he disapproves of, follows his principles but does not improve the world. To have an impact, all investors on the planet would have to have a similar zero tolerance policy. This is evidently not the case. Even among socially responsible investors, some do not want to hurt their portfolios' financial performance. For this reason, Guy's decision to ban "sin industries" from his investments, however idealistic, remains toothless.

Another Advantage of the Industry-Agnostic Approach

Companies might not change their lines of business, but they might change the way they do business if they see a realistic chance of attracting responsible investors. By selecting the most responsible companies in an industry, the industry-agnostic approach creates such a reward.

Advocates argue that using industry-agnostic screens creates powerful incentives for all companies to improve their responsibility standards and that industry exclusion does not have this effect, since companies from "sin" sectors are banned without any possibility of "appeal." If you give them a chance to be included by getting a higher SRI rating, you give them a reason to improve. You create competition among companies in the same industry to avoid being among the least responsible in their class.

Companies in sin sectors are not all equally noxious for society. While one alcohol company launches a seductive marketing campaign to increase sales to the younger population, another does so by also providing information on the negative effects of alcohol. Most people would agree they shouldn't be treated the same way. The industry-agnostic approach takes this fact into consideration and promotes the better companies as role models for that industry.

Still, some investors are troubled by seeing SRI portfolios investing in some "sin" industries. They believe that abandoning zero tolerance toward sin industries is a compromise that defeats the purpose of SRI—to punish firms that are not good for society and drive them to bankruptcy. That these firms would not be driven to bankruptcy makes the industry-agnostic approach more pragmatic.

In the history of SRI, this moral debate is an old one. Yale University, one of the first institutions to address formally the ethical responsibilities of institutional investors, organized an internal study group in 1969 that led to the publication of *The Ethical Investor*.[11] In this book, the moral dilemma of a responsible investor is clearly stated:

> The question whether one ought to seek moral purity or moral effectiveness in public action arises in the context of investment policy: should a university or other investor sell the stock of a company whose policies it finds morally abhorrent, or should it retain its shares and attempt to change the policies of that company? To some extent, this choice reflects the difference between the Kantians and the Utilitarians,

between those who judge the goodness of an act on the basis of its conformity to principle and those who judge the goodness of an act according to its effect.[12]

Another dimension of this debate has to do with whether it is enough to exclude companies with "concerns" or whether one should be more selective and invest in companies that not only are free of "concerns" but also exhibit some "strength" in their responsibility ratings. In other words, should one favor excellence over a decent standard? This concrete question about portfolio formation has to do with one's ultimate goal in practicing SRI. Is it to promote a global minimum standard for the behavior of companies and convince the laggards to comply with this minimum standard? Or is it to reward excellence, promoting the innovations of a few companies? In the first case, the recipe we have given here for investing in "no-concern" companies provides a satisfactory answer.

The industry-agnostic approach encourages all companies to care about their impact on society and the environment. It provides them with incentives to avoid being laggards on any value dimension. It creates a standard of decency—a minimum standard. Ask yourself how you would like firms to be in 10 years. If your vision for the future is one in which all companies respect minimum responsibility standards on several core dimensions, regardless of their line of business, then this form of SRI can contribute to your goal.

One potential critique is that this future might lead us to a gray zone where most companies indeed fulfill some minimum standard but excellence along certain responsibility dimensions is not rewarded. To avoid such a scenario, responsible investors might want to raise the bar higher by further narrowing down their portfolios. They might want to pursue their vision by holding firms that are exemplary rather than simply exempt of "concerns" in the issue areas they care about. What do we expect the financial performance of such a strategy to be? Is it the best way to promote faster progress in company's behavior? To answer this, we need to understand the financial performance of exemplary corporate citizens and analyze the effect of tighter screening on financial products. This is the topic of the next chapter.

Values *and* Increased Profits?

▨▨▨▨ Can Responsibility Increase Returns?

For many, the conclusion that SRI can offer competitive returns is surprising enough—imagine their reaction to this statement on the website of the UN Principles for Responsible Investment: "There is a growing view among investment professionals that environmental, social and corporate governance (ESG) issues can [positively] affect the performance of investment portfolios. Investors fulfilling their fiduciary (or equivalent) duty therefore need to give appropriate consideration to these issues."[1] In other words, SRI could potentially increase one's returns. Many socially responsible funds do advertise SRI as a way to boost returns; but advertising is one thing, and a statement from the United Nations is another. Are such statements overly optimistic? While it has not been definitively proven, there is much evidence suggesting that SRI can in fact boost portfolio returns.

How Corporate Responsibility Impacts Corporate Profits

Several rationales have been proposed to explain why social responsibility would lead to increased rather than decreased corporate profits. Traditional reasons that supporters of corporate social responsibility advocate include the following:

- *Employee loyalty and morale*: In companies with exemplary worker conditions and rights, employee retention and morale will be higher. This will translate into higher productivity.
- *Customer loyalty*: Irresponsible companies, due to their "misbehaviors," face the risk of consumer boycotts, loss of brand value, and having fewer repeat customers. All this eventually hurts sales and hence profits.
- *Legal risk*: Companies that violate social norms are likely to face higher litigation costs resulting from lawsuits individuals bring or penalties governments impose for violating existing regulations.

While a significant amount of empirical research has found support for such arguments, many studies show these effects being concentrated in specific industries. For example, in industries that involve direct interaction with consumers, such as retail, customer loyalty becomes important. Ray Fisman, Geof Heal and Vinay Nair (2006) found that social responsibility is correlated with higher profits, especially in industries where the firm image is important and advertising is pervasive.

As for the positive effect of being employee friendly, Alex Edmans, professor of finance at the Wharton School, has found that firms selected by *Fortune* in 1998 as the most employee-friendly exhibited higher profit growth than their industry peers over the next decade. (Edmans finds an annualized difference of 2.5%.) This evidence is in line with the fact that people rather than physical assets are at the core of the new business environment in which companies compete. Today, quality, creativity, and innovation, much more than machines, are the important assets. People make the value of firms, especially in research and development–intensive industries.

Concerning regulation, recent academic research shows that a company's regulatory problems can be predicted by using appropriate environmental and social information. This is especially true, of course, for companies in highly regulated sectors. For example, Aaron K. Chatterji at Duke University, David Levine at Berkeley University, and Michael Toffel at Harvard University examined information produced by the social rating company KLD Analytics. They show that "firms with more KLD concerns have slightly, but statistically significantly, more pollution and regulatory compliance violations in later years."[2]

The Issue of Employee Safety Affects a Takeover Battle

In January 2006, the global steel conglomerate Mittal Steel, run by India native Lakshmi Mittal, launched a hostile takeover bid for Arcelor, a European steel company with historical roots in France and headquarters in Luxembourg. Trying to fight the takeover and rally public opinion as well as political support, Arcelor's CEO, Guy Dollé, raised doubts about Mittal's willingness and ability to maintain high safety standards for its employees. He dramatically claimed that "whereas Arcelor's accident rate had fallen by 75 percent in the past four years, the accident rate at a former Arcelor plant in France now owned by Mittal had soared 10-fold."[3] Mittal responded in the newspaper *Les Echos:* "The history of our group was built with our employees. Our philosophy is to seek to maintain the highest standards in the fields of health, durable growth and safety. Our operations in France already bear out this point."[4] In a document aimed at Arcelor's shareholders entitled "Mittal, the Natural Alliance,"

(continued)

Mittal described the codified health and safety policy Mittal Steel had introduced in 2005, demonstrating the company's commitment to surpassing legal requirements in every country where it operates and backing the statements with quotations from several union representatives from Mittal Steel plants in Europe and the United States.[5] Dollé's accusations failed to gain credibility over the next months. For instance, French economist Nicolas Véron wrote in February 2006 in *La Tribune* that work conditions in Europe-based plants acquired by Mittal in 1999 were objectively not worse than those of plants belonging to European companies. [6] In June 2006, Arcelor's board finally accepted the acquisition by Mittal Steel. This example illustrates how responsibility standards can affect a company's ability to acquire firms in other countries.

While there is some empirical support for the link between social responsibility, and profits, the evidence for a very strong effect is not overwhelming. The responsibility-profit nexus appears to be industry-specific. David Vogel, in *The Market for Virtue*, summarizes the findings on whether "there is a business case for virtue." He shares a similar view and states that the claim of a relationship between profitability and responsibility "must be more nuanced. CSR [corporate social responsibility] does make business sense for some firms in specific circumstances." Moreover, many studies can be criticized for a hardly avoidable "chicken-and-egg" problem common in empirical economics: Do companies perform well because they are responsible or (like individuals) are they responsible because they are doing well and therefore can afford to behave in ways their peers cannot?[7]

If indeed the evidence for these traditional arguments about a positive link between profits and responsibility is not general enough or strong enough, why would professional investors make use of environmental and social information to pick stocks and increase their returns? Are there other reasons behind the claim of outperformance associated with SRIs?

Ted, our symbolic red investor, is a trader at a small hedge fund. His task is to select stocks that will generate high returns—companies whose share prices will go up more quickly than those of their competitors.

A Short Take on Short Selling

When mutual fund managers and individual investors believe a company's stock price will fall, they avoid buying that stock. When hedge fund managers believe the same, they "short" the stock. This is how short selling works. A hedge fund trader who believes that the stock price of a company will fall from $10 to $9 in a month borrows the stock from somebody who holds it, with a commitment to return it a month later. Right after borrowing, she sells the stock, for $10. If her prediction is right, she can buy the stock a month later for $9 and return it to the lender. She makes a profit of $1.

In order to do this, he gathers large amounts of information about companies, looking at everything from financial performance and industry trends to corporate strategy and management turnover. Over the years, he has developed a unique ability to quickly form a view about a company's outlook from a variety of different sources. He speaks with experts and managers to get a picture of where an industry is going and how its strategy fits this evolution. On the basis of his personal synthesis of all this information, he comes up with a prediction of a company's or industry's future profits. If a company trades at a price below what Ted believes is the "fair price," he buys it and expects good news to follow and increase the price. When he anticipates that a company is in for one or more bad surprises, he can also make money by betting the stock price will go down—in Wall Street parlance, he "shorts" such stocks (see sidebar).

This process of selecting stocks and betting they will go up or down is Ted's strategy. *He doesn't care much about "ethical investment" per se.* His job is to make money for the few, but large, investors who are his clients. His philosophy is simple: "Whatever is legal is ethical." Yet he uses some environmental, social and governance (ESG) information in his analysis. Why? Using environmental issues as an example, Ted explains:

> A consensus has now emerged in the scientific community on global warming. The issue has also captured public attention. After all, in 2007 Al Gore received the Nobel Peace Prize for educating and warning the public on the issue. It's pretty clear that regulation on environmental issues will get tighter. So companies that have started thinking about cleaning their production process and consuming less energy will have an edge. The laggards will have to do that in a rush, which means at a higher cost.

Ted is not the only one with this view. A survey of senior executives in the United States provides some guidance on future regulation.[8] Seven out of ten executives said they expect increased regulation of companies for environmental responsibility within the next five years. About 30% of them expected the same for social issues.

A tangible sign that more regulation is on its way is that large banks are starting to organize the market for pollution rights in the United States. As Blythe Masters, the chief financial officer of JPMorgan Chase, says about climate-related regulatory risk, "the most dangerous position to be in is one of ignorance."[9]

It's this difference between the ignorant and the prepared that Ted is trying to detect by looking at corporate actions. Michael E. Porter and Forest L. Reinhardt of Harvard University share his view:

Climate change is now a fact of political life and is playing a growing role in business competition. Greenhouse gas emissions will be increasingly scrutinized, regulated, and priced. While individual managers can disagree about how immediate and significant the impact of climate change will be, companies need to take action now. Companies that persist in treating climate change solely as a corporate social responsibility issue, rather than a business problem, will risk the greatest consequences.[10]

"ESG information is also a useful radar for evaluating managerial skills," Ted continues. "Indirectly, they help me evaluate some core aspects of a company's strategy. Take a CEO who knows that he is unlikely to remain in his position in a year. Well…that guy won't probably have strong incentives to invest in social and environmental initiatives that will pay off in a few years from now."

Ted is trying to infer how healthy a company is by looking at executive actions on long-term projects. He asks himself: Is the CEO overemphasizing short-term projects? Maybe the CEO knows something that makes him think short term. Perhaps the firm is doing worse than investors think. This view is echoed by Amy Domini, one of the founders of the leading social rating firm, KLD.

So why the long-term success? Those of us within the social investment industry know that the research process is extremely detailed and paints a particularly telling story of a corporation. The underlying culture and the quality of management emerge through the research process. At the end of the day, I believe that this is what has led to the overall out performance of KLD's Domini 400 Social Index vs. the S & P 500. We have based the portfolio toward high quality management teams and companies with strong and positive corporate cultures. These are widely viewed as highly important to corporate performance and extremely difficult to identify. Socially SRI, through its screening methodology, has found a way to identify these important factors.

Ted summarizes his views: "Whether they are making a mistake by underinvesting in long-term projects or whether they know something about future performance, I don't want to buy that company. I can sometimes detect a bad situation before the market even realizes something is going on."

Clearly, Ted's attitude toward SRI differs from those of values-based investors such as Kathy, Sven, and Guy. Ted invests in a responsible company only if he believes that social responsibility will give a boost to that company's future profits. His reasons for justifying the responsibility-profits link are different from the traditional reasons mentioned earlier. But they are important.

More and more mainstream professional managers and company analysts who keep an eye on environmental and social issues are coming to believe that social responsibility matters for future stock returns. They give credit to the view that companies that have a long-term strategy concerning environmental and social issues will be able to retain their competitive advantage while also being more agile in capturing new growth options and adapting to regulatory changes.

This widespread acknowledgment of the importance of environmental and social information in predicting companies' profits prompted the president of SRI World Group to comment that "a tectonic shift in investor consciousness—spurred in large part by widespread recognition of the dire implications of climate change—made 2006 the year of green investing.

Whereas investors previously viewed environmentalism as a drag on returns, they're now seeing green in all senses of the word when they look at windmills, solar panels, and biofuels."

The Worldwide Wave of Environmental Regulation Tightening

Following the UN-supported Kyoto Protocol, which entered into force February 16, 2005, the European Union has committed to cutting its emissions by 8% from 1990 levels by 2012. Each nation has taken on individual limits, for a total of 12,000 energy-intensive industrial plants. Industries constrained by the new regulation include power generation, iron and steel, glass, and cement. All in all, about 40% of the EU's total CO_2 emissions originate from the industries covered by the agreement

In response to increased concern about global warming, in 2007 the EU organized an energy summit, which adopted two binding targets to be met by 2020: reducing EU emissions by 20%, and having 20% of the EU's overall energy consumption come from renewable sources. These targets will translate into tighter legislation at the national level. They will also provide momentum in the search for innovative technologies and alternative sources for energy. A legislative framework to reduce CO_2 emissions from new cars and vans is in the pipeline, and taxing plane emissions is a topic in discussion.

The U.S. government, after being less receptive than the EU to environmental concerns and the need for regulation (it refused to ratify the Kyoto Protocol), is now getting more proactive. A sign of this shift is a July 2007 draft report published by the National Petroleum Council, an advisory body to the U.S. government, under the leadership of former ExxonMobil chief executive Lee R. Raymond. The report recommends five "core strategies" to "assist markets in meeting the energy challenges to 2030 and beyond." These include moderating demand growth by "increasing efficiency in transportation, residential,

(continued)

commercial and industrial uses" and reducing emissions of global warming gases by establishing a transparent, predictable, economy-wide cost for CO2 emissions and a regulatory framework for carbon sequestration and storage.* At the state level, regulation is already catching up. In 2006 California passed an act targetting a 25% reduction in carbon emissions by 2020. New York, New Jersey, Minnesota, Washington, Oregon, and Hawaii have passed similar laws. Three bills in the U.S. Senate and two in the House of Representatives are pressing for federal reduction targets. (*From "Facing the Hard Truths about Energy," report from the National Petroleum Council, July 2007, available at http://www.npchardtruthsreport.org.)

Several mainstream investment analysts now issue investing reports that incorporate environmental and social factors. Innovest, created in 1995, has become a major provider of company-level nonfinancial information. According to Innovest,

> companies' ability to handle political, environmental, labor, and human rights risks are powerful proxies and leading indicators for their overall management quality—or the lack thereof. Generating superior returns requires accurately anticipating changes in companies' competitive prospects before the broader market recognizes them. We believe that optimal investment results require combining robust "extra-financial" analysis with more traditional fundamental, quantitative, and qualitative approaches.[11]

Another example: Goldman Sachs, one of Wall Street's leading firms, recently released a report that recommends 44 companies on the basis of the combination of ESG screens and financial information. Like other empirical studies, this report insists that ESG relevance for profits is highly industry-specific.

Our conclusion is that companies need to manage all inputs to their business in order to enjoy sustained competitive advantage and a valuation premium versus their peers. What is more profound, perhaps, is that investors cannot rely on ESG factors alone but need to integrate them into an industrial framework and valuation methodology to pick stocks.... [This report's] focus list members have to rank well on a combination of ESG score and industry positioning. This must then translate into improving financial performance and, ultimately, returns.[12]

Regulation Tightening Affects Auto Industry Profits in Europe

The European Commission is currently insisting that by 2012, the fleet-average emissions from new cars sold in the EU must not exceed 130 g/km. According to a recent article in the *Economist*, "although it will be at least a year before they become law and there is still scope for some of the details to change—both the European Parliament and the Council of Ministers will want their say—there is now little doubt that in only a few years' time European carmakers will have to meet the world's strictest CO_2-emission standards."[13] The article shows that all car manufacturers are not equally impacted by this new law (see fig. 4.1). Some have anticipated this regulatory evolution by substantially decreasing their CO_2 emission levels in recent years.

The French and the Italians, represented by PSA Peugeot Citroën, Renault and Fiat, have so far been fairly sanguine. In 2006 their fleets, heavily biased towards fuel-efficient small cars, averaged 142–147 g/km. It will not be easy for them to meet the new rules without increasing the cost of their cheap, low-margin cars, but they are close enough to be confident that they can get there.... For the Germans it is a different matter.... As things stand, the Germans have no hope of avoiding substantial fines unless they are given longer to comply and are prepared to change their mix of models. Neither looks likely.[14]

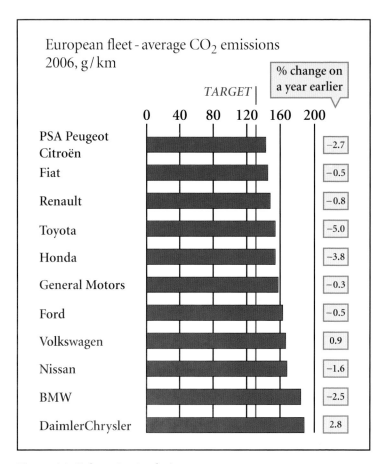

Figure 4.1 Exhaustive Analysis.
Source: Institute for European Environmental Policy.

Evidence for Corporate Responsibility
Boosting Stock Returns

Ted, like Innovest and the authors of the Goldman Sachs report, thinks that the stock market is a bit slow in realizing the scope of environmental and social actions. Since factors relating to social responsibility are "intangibles" that are absent from financial reports, and because they affect future profits and not only current profits, it is possible that the market overlooks their importance.

If the benefits of social responsibility for companies are indeed higher than generally recognized, then selecting responsible firms will generate higher returns, because the market will only reward *in several months* the responsibility standards that companies are adopting *today*.

There is some evidence that such "sluggish repricing" of responsible companies has been taking place lately. The Goldman Sachs report substantiates this by showing that a portfolio that used what it calls the "GS Sustain" methodology historically outperformed benchmark portfolios. Using Innovest data, Jeroen Derwall, a finance professor at Erasmus University, and his colleagues (2005) found significant overperformance of high-ecofriendly companies over low-ecofriendly ones. Controlling for the usual risk factors, such as market performance, the over-performance was about 5% a year, the researchers found.[15]

Some other studies confirm that in the recent years, the most conscious companies have tended to have higher returns. Recently, Edmans found that investing in the 163 firms that *Fortune* selected in January 1998 as the "Best Companies to Work For in America…earned more than double the market return by the end of 2005."[16] Even after controlling for traditional risk factors, Edmans finds for this portfolio a monthly premium of 0.64%.[17] He concludes that SRI need not decrease returns.

We ran our own analysis. Following the recipe presented in chapter 3, we constructed a portfolio of "superresponsible" companies by selecting firms from the S & P 500. Using KLD ratings, we investigated their actions in the three areas of the environment, customers (product safety), and employee treatment. The firms we selected had strengths in at least one of the three areas and no weaknesses in any of them. We then compared these responsible firms with all the firms in the S & P 500. Our superresponsible portfolio had approximately 100 companies; our comparison portfolio, the S & P 500, had 500 companies. But the lack of diversification didn't appear to have a cost in term of risk and returns. The superresponsible portfolio had a monthly return of 0.62% over 1999–2007, more than the S & P 500 average return (.41%) and more than the "zero-concern" portfolio of chapter 3. Despite having fewer firms (100 vs. 200), the superresponsible portfolio was not more volatile than the zero-concern portfolio. (Both had a volatility of 0.042.) Clearly, these 100 firms were good enough performers to make up for the lack of diversification.[18]

The outperformance of highly responsible companies in the last few years is a fact. It explains the high level of interest on the part of asset managers.

▐ ▌■ ■   Is the Party Over?

How long can such outperformance continue? The studies that have documented historical outperformance of socially responsible portfolios warn that past performance does not guarantee future returns. The idea behind this warning is that people like Ted buy the stock if its price is lower than its *fair value*—the value that takes into account profits expected in the future and accounts for the risk in these estimations. Wall Street is populated by thousands of people like Ted. As they buy such stocks, the prices rise and soon reflect the fair value. Once prices of responsible companies catch up with their fair levels, they will no longer outperform their peers.

The Efficient Markets Paradigm versus Behavioral Finance

According to the theory of efficient markets, formalized by the work of University of Chicago professor Eugene Fama, stock prices should reflect immediately all available information on a company's future profits. There should be no discrepancy between the "market value" of a company (the combined value of its stocks) and its "fundamental value" (the value of its future profits). A consequence is that it should be impossible to predict whether stock prices will go up or down on the basis of currently available information.[19]

However, in the last two decades, systematic deviations from the efficient market view (called market anomalies) have been documented. It is more commonly admitted that the convergence of prices toward their fundamental value is not instantaneous but takes time, because of market frictions that limit the size and horizon of the trades that arbitrageurs (such as hedge funds) can make.[20] In addition, some investors might not process information in a purely rational manner: depending of the focus of their attention, they tend to overweight or underweight certain pieces of information, and they are subject to "market sentiment."[21] The trades of these investors can push stock prices away from their fundamental value.

We believe responsible portfolios will continue to outperform benchmark portfolios. And this future outperformance is likely to come from *the unexpected acceleration of SRI investments*. We expect a strong acceleration in the number of investors joining the "best-in-class" SRI crowd, an acceleration that goes beyond what the market is expecting.

The increase in responsible capital is likely to make SRI investment cross a critical threshold: Given the increase in the proportion of investors who apply SRI screens, we expect that highly responsible companies will in the future be able to raise capital at a slightly lower cost than their peers. Everything else being equal, a company that has to pay less to raise capital is worth more, as it can invest in new projects at a lower cost. So, as this effect will get noticed, it will translate into higher stock-returns. Even though we expect the cost of capital to change only by a small amount, the scope of this trend is powerful. For this reason, there is a fair chance that the party might just be beginning.

We usually side with the skeptics when it comes to market anomalies and easy profits. Are we talking about minuscule numbers, or is this "cost of capital effect" substantial? Here's a quick "back-of-the-envelope" calculation. Professors Robert Heinkel, Alan Kraus, and Josef Zechner (from the University of British Columbia and the University of Vienna) show that if the amount of SRI capital switches from 10% of the total available capital to 15% in three years, the cost of capital of responsible companies is lowered by a little more than 0.8%, compared to that of their less responsible peers.[22] For example, imagine that the returns that responsible companies have to promise to their investors switches from 10% to 9.2% because of the rise of responsible capital. A conservative estimate is that the value of those companies should increase, due to that effect alone, by 11%.[23]

This means that a portfolio of responsible companies will outperform a comparable portfolio of less responsible companies by 11%. If this increase in the fraction of SRI capital occurs within the next three to five years, we are talking about an annual premium of 2.2% to 3.7% during the transition. Investors like

Ted, who can buy responsible firms and short less responsible ones, can exploit this. Small investors like Kathy, Sven, and Guy, who cannot easily short companies, have less to gain. If the less responsible firms make up 10% of the entire market value of companies, by avoiding them in an index, one would outperform an all-inclusive index (such as the S & P 500) by 1.1% of this period—an annual benefit of 0.22% to 0.37%.

If we are more optimistic and assume the SRI capital fraction crosses the 20% threshold within five years, as our analysis indicates it will, the repricing effect would then be more than double that amount (22%). This would translate into an annual premium of 4.5–7.3% for Ted and 0.45–0.73% for Kathy, Guy, and Sven.

For the sake of being conservative, let us assume that the repricing effect is only half of the Heinkel-Kraus-Zechner estimate and that the fraction of SRI capital increases by 50% over five years. Then SRI overperformance would still be above 1% annualized over the next five years. Investing $10,000 for five years at a 10% return rather than a 9% return yields an extra $720. Is that worth thinking about?

Such repricing of companies in the context of SRI has a historical precedent. Social norms regarding tobacco changed dramatically during the 1960s. The surgeon general's report on smoking and health came out in 1964, and there was much reporting of the health hazards of smoking during the 1960s. In 1971, television ads for cigarettes were finally banned in the United States. During this period of change, several investors shunned tobacco stocks. To date, the elimination of tobacco companies remains the single most prevalent screen applied by several funds. It's encouraging to revisit the effect of this transition in social norms. Tobacco companies performed poorly between 1965 and 1970. But there was no such underperformance after 1970: At that point the stock-market had fully accounted for their increased cost of capital.

Will the acceleration of the growth of capital dedicated to SRI translate into high SRI returns for a few years? Yes—if the market does not fully anticipate the scope and consequences of the acceleration right away. Otherwise, prices would already reflect the consequences of the higher capital available to responsible companies.

Here is why we find this sluggish market reaction plausible. The academic literature in behavioral finance documents several instances in which stock prices deviate from "rational expectations" of future profits. On the basis of these results, we find it plausible that the market will take time to become aware that the scope of SRI is about to change and that this change will have an impact on companies' ability to generate profits.

Because the human brain uses heuristics, such as extrapolating the past to predict the future, people tend to realize only slowly that a regime switch has occurred. Several psychologists, including Ward Edwards, have described this sluggishness (in comparison to a fully rational individual) in updating beliefs in the face of new evidence, a phenomenon they call belief conservatism.[24] Many investors will therefore take time to fully take into account the consequences of an acceleration of the growth of SRI. Building on such psychological evidence, Nicholas Bareberis and his colleagues developed a model of what happens to stock prices in a market where investors underreact in the short run to new information.[25]

A Slow Repricing Precedent: Corporate Governance

A useful precedent for the kind of slow transition we have been discussing exists in the area of corporate governance. During the 1990s, following the acquisition frenzy and the disclosure scandals, the market progressively realized the performance impact of a company's corporate governance characteristics.

If a company has a "poison pill" (a mechanism that makes it costly for an investor to acquire a majority of shares in the company) and a staggered board (preventing a major renewal of board members), it becomes less vulnerable to takeovers. These companies are far from the corporate democracy model: managers are more entrenched and less likely to lose their jobs, and therefore feel less pressure. The board tends to be less challenging vis-à-vis the CEO, and on average, performance is lower. Three researchers, Paul Gompers, Joy L. Ishii, and Andrew Metrick, have constructed an index measuring how good a company is at corporate governance. When they looked at the performance of a "best-in-class" strategy along the corporate governance dimension, they found that buying firms in the best 10% of their corporate governance index (good governance) and selling firms in the worse 10% of the index (bad governance) would have earned risk-returns of 8.5% per year during the 1990s (these returns are net of the risks of the strategy, in other words they cannot be interpreted as a premium rewarding higher risk). It took a decade for the market to fully reflect the importance of corporate governance in companies' values.

There is also direct empirical evidence that stock markets tend to be slow at pricing the impact of predictable shocks to a company's future profits. For example, Stefano DellaVigna (of the University of California at Berkeley) and Joshua Pollet (of the University of Illinois at Urbana-Champaign) have shown that the stock prices of companies take time to reflect predictable future changes in the demand for their products. For example, if a lot of babies are to be born in a year, this would be good news for toy sales a few years down the road. In a "textbook" financial market, one would expect the stock prices of these companies to reflect the good news right away. In reality, it takes a few years for stock prices to fully reflect the predictable increase. So investors can make money by investing in these companies beforehand. DellaVigna and Pollet found that a trading strategy exploiting demographic information earns an annualized risk-adjusted return of approximately 6% a year.

To summarize, on the basis of academic evidence, we find it plausible that the market will only slowly realize the price impact of a quick acceleration of SRI.

▪▪▪ The Oncoming Big Wave

Our belief that SRI will continue providing above-standard returns in the coming years bears two conditions. First, as noted, one must invest while stock prices are not yet reflecting fully the impact on companies of the future increase in SRI assets. Second, a substantial acceleration of the growth of capital dedicated to SRI must happen within the next years.

We mentioned, as our reference scenario, an increase of the share of SRI capital from 10% to 20% of total assets. Is this expectation reasonable? We see nine mutually reinforcing trends that suggest that SRI capital, which is currently about 10% of the pool of capital, will indeed approach the 20% threshold within the next five years.

Trend 1: The Boom in Retail SRI

Already, SRI has deeply penetrated the space of public pension funds and endowments; now SRI is rapidly growing in mutual funds. As a large fraction of U.S. savings are invested in defined contribution plans, more individuals can choose SRI options. Already, about 19% of defined contribution plans offer an SRI option, and another 41% will do so within the next 2–3 years.[26] Partly in response to the demand, many mutual fund families now offer SRI options.

In addition, competition prompts mutual funds to offer such responsible products. These funds have slashed costs and try to differentiate themselves in areas different from returns. Social responsibility is a very natural marketing dimension for mutual funds, as it reinforces clients' trust in the managing company. A study by Fisman, Geoffrey Heal of Columbia University, and Nair (2006) argued that social responsibility is a powerful marketing strategy in industries where customer trust is important.[27] For example, if you buy organic food, you need to trust that the seller is indeed complying with the production constraints of organic food. You might be more inclined to trust a "socially responsible" organic food producer. The same argument applies to financial products; clients to feel safe putting their nest eggs into the fund family, they need to trust the risk management process and the integrity of the managing companies.

One of the earliest such options for individual investors was offered by TIAA-CREF, when it launched its CREF Social Choice Account in 1990. With nearly $9 billion in assets as of March 31, 2007, this account is the largest comprehensively screened investment vehicle for individual investors in the United States. The total share of SRI within TIAA-CREF is increasing, and at 2.3% in 2006, it still has ample room to grow.

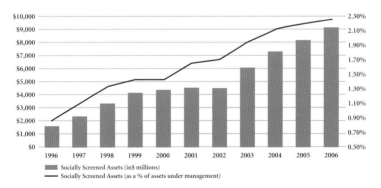

Figure 4.2 SRI at TIAA-CREF, 2006–2007.
Source: "Socially Responsible Investing at TIAA-CREF," Public Memo by TIAA-CREF, 2007, p. 3, available at www.tiaa-cref.org/about/press/about_us/releases/pdf/c40955.pdf.
*As of December 31, 2006. Socially screened assets include the CREF Social Choice Account, TIAA-CREF Institutional Social Choice Equity Fund, and TIAA-CREF Life Social Choice Equity Fund.

Two signs confirm the coming boom in the SRI retail market. First, a sign of retail demand is the proliferation of new green exchange traded funds (ETFs; baskets of stocks traded on the stock market). PowerShares (a market leader in ETFs) launched two index-based ETFs: the WilderShares Progressive Energy Portfolio (PUW) and the PowerShares Cleantech Portfolio (PZD). A second sign is the recent public listing of several environmentally conscious businesses. "Socially SRI demand far exceeds the supply of equity issues by renewable-energy companies," said John Lynch, managing director of the energy and power group at Merrill Lynch.[28]

Trend 2: New SRI Products Cost Less, so More People Join

As we discussed in chapter 3, for a long time, a strong argument of skeptics was that SRI diminishes diversification. By eliminating specific industries such as tobacco, SRI funds were hurting their performance in downturns. The current ongoing trend of replacing industry-specific negative screens with best-in-class screens is convincingly alleviating the diversification concern. As the cost in diversification of being an SRI investor is de facto becoming negligible, more and more investors are choosing to express their values through their investments.

An analogy can be drawn with voting behavior. As a citizen, you are likely to be interested in expressing your political opinion by voting in national or local elections. Imagine however that voting would take you a day of travel or an expensive travel fare, would you still pay the cost? Many citizens wouldn't. A recent academic study using U.S. turnout data shows that accessibility to the ballot makes a significant difference to turnout.[29] The authors use the fact that some precinct locations are more accessible than others, and hypothesize that "for the less accessible ones, at least some people will feel that the cost to get there outweighs any benefit they may reap in terms of personal satisfaction from having fulfilled a civic obligation." Even after controlling for variables that account for the motivation, information and resource levels of local precinct populations, they "find that accessibility does make a significant difference to turnout." Namely, "a five mile increase [in proximity] would produce a 2.3% increase in turnout."

We are entering a period where the cost of investing responsibly is becoming negligible. Like higher ballot accessibility, this will increase the "turnout" of investors choosing to express their values through their investment.

Trend 3: Standardization of Information

Several European countries now require companies to report information on environmental and social issues, several other countries are contemplating similar measures. Investor support for shareholder resolutions that demand companies to report their social and environmental performance is at a historical high. Following the higher demand from investors and regulatory constraints, companies are reporting nonfinancial information in a more standardized and credible manner. An indicator of this is that the percentage of Fortune Global 100 companies issuing sustainability reports increased from 48% in 2003 to 72% in 2004.[30] Most of these reports are audited as well. This standardization of information has helped many investors to incorporate social and environmental information into their decision-making process. It has also helped many SRI funds converge in their views of a company.

The following nonprofit initiatives are further accelerating the standardization of SRI information:

- The Carbon Disclosure Project is an independent lobbying organization that works with 315 institutional investors and surveys 2,400 of the world's largest companies about greenhouse gas emissions and changes in technology. "The latest Carbon Disclosure Report issued in September on the world's 500 largest publicly traded companies revealed that 77% of them had answered the questionnaire. Of these, 76% had initiated an emissions-reduction program, up from 48% in 2006."[31] According to Tessa Tennant, founder of the Association for Sustainable and Responsible Investment in Asia,, "There's nothing like peer-group pressure. For companies to see what their competitors are doing is a great spur to action."[32]

- The Global Reporting Initiative (GRI), a nonprofit organization collaborating with the UN Global Compact initiative, has developed a standard framework of reporting on environmental and social performance that has become the worldwide standard in sustainability reporting guidelines. According to Al Gore, "more transparency in reporting, as exemplified by the GRI, will help us more broadly 'price in' the external costs of investment decisions. This, in turn, will help enable capital markets to achieve their intended purpose—[to] consistently allocate capital to its highest and best use for people and the planet."[33]

Several rating agencies (in U.S. and Europe) with experience are providing information on corporate responsibility. Because investors can now rely on more homogeneous reporting from companies, these ratings have become more credible: the idea of ranking companies by responsibility in a given industry is now a feasible one.

Trend 4: Peer Effects in 401(k) Choices: Viral Propagation of SRI

There is evidence that strong peer effects at the workplace exist when it comes to 401(k) savings: people are deeply influenced by one another's choices. A few individuals in a firm can have a large impact on their colleagues' savings behavior. Esther Duflo and Emmanuel Saez showed the important role of social interactions in the employees' decisions to enroll in the 401(k) plan of a large university: a few informed individuals had a strong impact on their colleagues' behavior.[34]

Another study, by Massimo Massa (of INSEAD) and Andrei Simonov (of the Stockholm School of Economics), finds that investors tend to invest in the same stocks as their former classmates.[35] This suggests that once a critical mass has adopted it, an investment style such as SRI can spread in the population through peer interactions.

While most people have only a vague idea of how to make the best portfolio decisions, the current adopters of SRI typically have strong views about its importance. This makes it even more likely that early SRI enthusiasts will influence the decisions of a significant number of people with whom they interact. If this happens, SRI will have a strong "viral" aspect.

Trend 5: Sovereign Funds

The huge sovereign wealth funds (as discussed in chapter 1) are likely to become dominant players in global markets. By some estimates, the amount they control is currently $2.5 trillion and is likely to grow to $12 trillion by 2015. As these funds enter the markets, those of the democratic countries are expected to follow Norway's model. This brings a significant player into financial markets that invests public money and is more likely to be concerned about commonly accepted values.

For example (as noted in chapters 1 and 2), in 2004, after its first decade of activity, Norway's Government Pension Fund defined precise guidelines for its investment policy. This fund has reserves of more than $350 billion. Just including it in the SRI fraction of investors increases the amount of SRI capital invested from 1 in 10 dollars to 1 in 8.5! As noted in chapter 1, because it is so large and so credible, any divestment decision this fund makes on the basis of a company's failure to practice social responsibility will gain widespread public attention.

Trend 6: The UN Principles for Responsible Investment

These principles, intended to establish a common ground for SRI and define a set of universal values and guidelines around which investors can organize their responsibility policy, were published in 2006 (as noted in chapter 1). So far, more than $10 trillion of professionally managed assets have subscribed to the UN guidelines. This is another sign of the development of SRI.

Subscribing to the principles is aspirational: It does not mean all the funds who do so are already investing socially but that they commit to develop a process of SRI in the next few years. But investors who have subscribed to the PRI have to report to the UN Secretariat on what exactly they have been doing in the area, as is not the case for many other initiatives. This important detail makes the entire exercise more meaningful and not purely passive.

This is an encouraging signal of the future scope and size of SRI. If only half these subscribers go on to adopt SRI over the next three years, the amount of SRI capital would double, and SRI would become a mainstream investing approach

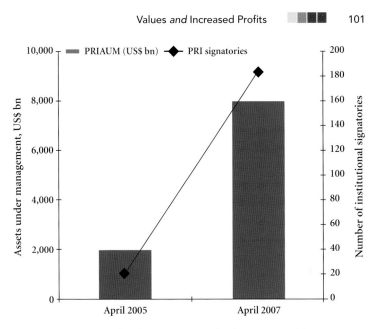

Figure 4.3 Support for the UN Principles for Responsible Investment.
Source: Goldman Sacs, "Introducing Goldman Sustain," public memo, June 22, 2007, p. 26, available at http://www.unglobalcompact.org/docs/summit2007/gs_esg_embargoed_until030707pdf.pdf.

used by large institutional asset managers rather than a niche market.

Trend 7: Responsible Firms Want to Offer Responsible Savings

As companies become more responsible, they will want their pension funds or 401(k) plans to be compatible with the values they try to express in their corporate behavior, so they will offer SRI options to their employees. And if responsibility is part of these firms' identities, their employees will also be more likely to adopt these options.

Trend 8: Toward Responsible Alternative Investments

Pension funds and endowments are increasingly investing in alternative investments such as hedge funds and private equity funds. As they come to favor funds that are congruent with their responsibility standards, one can expect a growing demand for responsible private equity and hedge funds. Such an evolution is just starting to be visible in the market place: In November 2007, the Swiss alternative investment adviser Harcourt joined forces with the Swedish insurance group Folksam and the Norwegian insurance group Storebrand to launch a socially responsible fund of hedge funds.

Total assets managed by hedge funds are currently estimated at $1.5 trillion. But because they leverage their positions by borrowing, hedge funds hold much more than this amount in U.S. companies, and account for more than half of the average trading volume in equity and corporate bond markets. They represent a category of investor that large public corporations will have to take into account more and more.

These trends indicate that the amount of capital utilizing social and environmental information should increase during the next three to five years, and responsible investors could benefit as a result of the consequent repricing.

Trend 9: The Professional Rise of Women

In a recent article on U.S. SRI, Steve Shueth relates the rise of SRI to the increasingly important place of women in corporate America and, consecutively, their more prominent role as investors and decision makers in household savings decisions:

> As women have moved out of the home and into the workforce, as they have filled the ranks of MBA programs, as they have worked their way up the ladder within large orga-

nizations. As they have taken seats on boards of directors and assumed roles as fiduciaries, women have brought a natural affinity to the concept of SRI with them. The social investment industry calculates that roughly 60% of socially conscious investors are women.[36]

There is direct empirical evidence that women tend to invest assets differently from men and typically put more weight on altruistic considerations and future generations. Other less direct evidence suggests the same. For example, the economist Esther Duflo, of the Massachusetts Institute of Technology, using results from a public program in South Africa, found that when public subsidies are given to women, they are invested on children's health, but that no such effect exists when subsidies are given to men.[37] For Duflo, "this suggests that the household does not function as a unitary entity" and that wealth will be invested differently depending on who earns it.

With the increase in wealth held by the women of the world and with their decision-making power, we expect preferences for social responsibility to increase.

Malcolm Gladwell, author of the best-seller *Tipping Point*, explains that the expression "tipping point" "comes from the world of epidemiology. It's the name given to that moment in an epidemic when a virus reaches critical mass. It's the boiling point. It's the moment on the graph when the line starts to shoot straight upwards." (Quoted from Malcolm Gladwell's website at http://www.gladwell.com.)

All these factors point toward an increase in the scope of SRI in the coming years. Its adoption is also mutually rein-forcing. More institutions joining will boost the returns of SRI portfolios, which will make even more investors interested in

SRI. More people being interested in SRI increases demand for high-quality responsibility ratings, which in turn help make SRI more credible. This snowball effect has begun, and is unlikely to reverse. Once it passes beyond the "tipping point," the positive feedback loops we have mentioned make it likely that SRI could become a mainstream phenomenon. As this transition occurs, the returns of SRI investors will be abnormally high. There will no conflict between returns and values. On the contrary, one will imply the other.

Is SRI Sustainable?

Many mainstream money managers who first came across SRI considered it a fad. The growing interest in SRI has brought new players and views into SRI, but for many a question remains. *Has SRI simply grown into a more powerful craze or is it truly sustainable?*

Doubtful investors who believe that incorporating a particular set of "values" in investment might well be the "flavor of the month" will not be interested in joining the SRI movement. Such investors will find it difficult to believe that companies' behavior will really change in response to something that is a passing trend. They also fear that SRI portfolios will be hurt once the fad disappears, since their stocks will then lose any associated premium.

We see this concern about SRI as a legitimate and important one to address if the movement is to grow further.

After all, fads are not restricted to the world of fashion. Here's an example from the world of finance. In 2001, three finance professors at Purdue University wrote an article showing a strong positive stock market reaction to companies that added

".com" to their company names.[1] The article identified about 100 such name changes made between 1998 and 1999 (mostly by small companies) and found dramatic increases in the companies' stock market value following their name changes. What was striking was that this increase did not depend on the company's level of involvement with the internet. This "dot-com" effect produced cumulative abnormal returns of 74% after the announcement day and did not appear to be transitory. After the internet "crash" of mid-2000, the trend reversed. Firms with ".com" in their names started trading at a discount, not a premium. This reversal motivated a sequel article by the same authors, who showed that after the crash, investors started reacting positively to firms that had *removed* ".com" from their names! "This ... deletion effect produces cumulative abnormal returns on the order of 64 percent for the sixty days surrounding the announcement day." They concluded that "investors are potentially influenced by cosmetic effects."[2]

So financial markets can be subject to fads and the power of cosmetic marketing. Moreover, as the example shows, surfing such fads can backfire, as stocks' values can fall dramatically when a fad comes to an end.

▨■■■ Assessing What Form of SRI Is Sustainable

The example highlights that the skeptics are not irrational pessimists, and brings us to the critical question: How can SRI be truly sustainable? To determine the answer, we need to look into two aspects of SRI: first, the issues that are of concern, and second, investors' motivations.

Different issues. To address whether SRI is sustainable, we must break down the notion of SRI to a specific issue. Several issue areas can be expressed in SRI, and some might be more sustainable than others. Some areas might be fads, and others might not. Thus, as it stands today, SRI might be sustainable along several dimensions and at the same time be a fad along others. So we need to talk of each issue specifically when we address the sustainability question.

Different investor motivations. Because the concern about SRI's sustainability is ultimately about the sustainability of *demand* for it, it is important to distinguish between the various motivations that bring different investors into the SRI space.

To show what these differences in issues and in motivations imply about SRI's sustainability, we will take the approach that for each single issue, SRI is a mix of the three investor preferences we have designated yellow, blue, and red.

A Reminder: What Color Is Your Investment Approach?

Yellow investors feel morally obliged to avoid companies that are incompatible with some of their values. They believe that doing otherwise would be immoral. Their decision to invest responsibly is quite insensitive to what it might cost them and to the impact on companies' behavior. Guy, the investor in chapter 3 who wanted all his money invested into socially responsible funds, is a yellow investor.

Blue investors are pragmatic. They are only interested in SRI if they are convinced that it can change the world in the direction of their values and that the financial cost is small. Kathy and Sven in chapters 1 and 2 are both blue investors.

Red investors are not motivated by moral concerns. They believe there are profits to be made from investing in responsible companies because they will outperform their peers in the coming years. Ted, the professional fund manager in chapter 4, is a red investor.

Investment interest in every issue starts off at an initial level: the sum of the amounts invested by all the yellow, blue, and red investors who initially express interest in the issue in their portfolio holdings. This initial level of interest is important to predicting the sustainability of SRI regarding this issue.

Among these initial investments, the core fraction of capital is the one that represents a core group of yellow investors—such as Guy—with respect to the issue. The level of SRI dedicated to an issue will never fall below this core level, as these yellow investors feel obliged to take the issue into account in their investments.

When many skeptics dismiss SRI as a fad, they are often implicitly stating that yellow investors will not keep increasing or grow into a large pool. We agree that if the sustainability of SRI is solely dependent on yellow investors, these SRI doubters are right.

However, as we have shown, the investment capital comes from not only the yellow but the blue and red investors, too. They all have different reasons for their actions, but at the end of the day, their actions may all be in harmony. So to properly assess the sustainability of an SRI issue, we need to add the support it receives from blue and red investors to its yellow support.

What determines blue and red support? Is it fickle and temporary? Here is where the sustainability of SRI is determined.

▮▮▮▮▮ SRI Goes Mainstream

The sustainability of SRI for a specific issue depends on how many blue investors will join the core group of yellow ones. Blue investors need to be convinced that investor pressure about the issue *both* will effectively improve corporate behavior *and* will not significantly hurt their portfolio returns. So how and when does a committed kernel of yellow believers in a given SRI issue snowball into a large group of mainstream blue and red investors?

First of all, the support the yellow investors receive from blue ones depends on whether that support is likely to have an impact. Blue investors will not adopt impractical or unrealistic issues—for example, pressuring a firm to change its line of business. If a change cannot be executed at some reasonable cost, blue investors are not willing to consider the next step. They know "it just won't happen," and they think of other more useful ways to express their values. This kind of cause is then likely to remain a fad—that is, as noted, the yellow investors will not keep increasing or grow into a large pool. If a demanded change can be fulfilled in a reasonable manner, blue investors may entertain the thought of supporting the issue through their investments.

These blue investors might have a range of different perceptions of whether the issue is a big step or a small step forward for the kind of change they want to achieve, but share the view that it is a positive change and are all willing to take the next step: looking at financial performance. Remember that blue investors do not want to bear significant financial costs to support the yellow ones. Some of them will clearly be willing to bear more than others, but as a whole they will care about these costs.

If the starting level of interest in the issue—all the yellow investors and a few less return-sensitive blue investors—is 10% of the total capital invested in the stock-market, the movement can snowball as follows. As we have shown, a significant minority of investors can get firms to pay attention. Managers will consider what they can do to prevent their company from being "banished" from the portfolios of this group of investors, especially as they are known to be loyal investors. So some firms will change. They will be those firms for which the cost of complying with the cause is relatively low and the benefit from access to long-term shareholders is relatively high.

This will have two consequences. First, many blue investors, having witnessed a change, will be more confident about the impact their investment can make. This will draw them to adopting this issue in their investment approach. They will be more prone to give SRI a chance.

Second, as some firms change, the number of "delinquent" firms decreases. Fewer firms are now excluded from a portfolio that is responsible with regard to this issue, and financial performance is therefore less likely to be compromised: A portfolio that excludes delinquent firms becomes less unattractive. Indeed, as we showed in chapter 3, the concerns about the performance of SRI stems from its lack of diversification. If fewer companies are excluded, this concern fades away. This will further attract more blue investors.

The level of capital will thus climb higher than the initial 10%. A higher level of capital will now pressure more firms to change, setting in motion a snowballing effect as more and more blue investors join the yellow investors and more and more firms adopt the standards demanded.

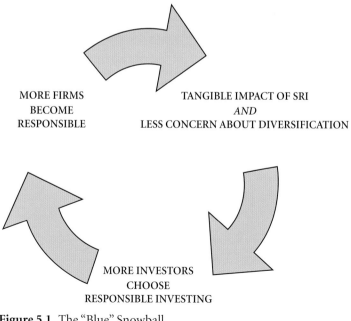

MORE FIRMS
BECOME
RESPONSIBLE

TANGIBLE IMPACT OF SRI
AND
LESS CONCERN ABOUT DIVERSIFICATION

MORE INVESTORS
CHOOSE
RESPONSIBLE INVESTING

Figure 5.1 The "Blue" Snowball.

The Economics of Social Interactions

The "virtuous circle" of the "blue snowball" (see fig. 5.1) belongs to a class of phenomena economists call "social externalities" or "social interactions." Professor Jose Scheinkman of Princeton University defines social interactions as "particular forms of externalities, in which the actions of a reference group affect an individual's preferences."[3] If people are more inclined to perform an action when many other people are performing it, small changes in the economic or social background can lead to large changes in the number of people performing the action. This type of economic analysis has been successfully used to illuminate phenomena as different as economic growth, adoption of innovations, racial segregation, desertions from armies, and crime.

For example, when the number of people being victimized by criminal activities in a neighborhood increases, the police and legal system tend to be saturated, which decreases the chances of punishment for criminals. This represents a change in incentives such that the number of people who become criminals tends to increase further.[4] Using FBI and New York City Police Department data, Professors Glaeser, Sacerdote, and Scheinkman (of Harvard University, Dartmouth College, and Princeton University, respectively) have shown that such social interaction effects are "highest in petty crimes, moderate in more serious crimes and almost negligible in murder and rape."[5]

What about the red investors (those interested exclusively in profits)? At different points, different red investors, such as Ted, will join the trend in anticipation of the movement of blue investors. They anticipate that the growth in capital that is chasing the companies that are responding positively to the issue will drive their stock prices up. They join the movement in order to profit from this upswing. So during this snowballing period, yellow, blue and red investors will all be involved.

■■■■■   Asking for Realistic Changes

Socially responsible investing involves a collection of issues. Some of them are skeptically—and sometimes correctly—viewed as trends that will reach a plateau before going mainstream. These issues involve the pursuit of unreasonable demands on firms.

Screening out tobacco is a striking example. The number of yellow investors who do this is high—high enough that a large fraction of SRI portfolios have been removing all firms doing any tobacco business. The yellow investors' goal regarding this issue is a moral one, namely avoiding to profit from an industry they condemn. This issue has been expensive for many tobacco firms; for more than 30 years they have faced a higher cost of capital than companies in other industries. But that has hardly wiped them out; tobacco companies still exist. Many blue investors remain invested in this sector because they see little impact from the yellow investors' pressure and, at least in recessions, significant financial costs of leaving the sector. Blue investors' lack of support for the issue leaves the red investors out as well. Red investors would only abandon tobacco companies if they expected a significant fraction of blue investors to do so in the future, pushing the value of tobacco firms down. Notwithstanding that possibility, the support for abandoning tobacco stocks has reached a plateau. The yellow investors are numerous enough to be noticeable, but the issue is not sustainable, because it is unlikely to appeal to mainstream (red and blue) investors.

Indeed, it is doubtful that tobacco screens can provoke the snowballing process we have just described. Blue investors know that realistically, tobacco companies won't disappear. And these investors are not willing to compromise their portfolio diversification for the sake of a lost cause. They would rather give money to subsidize nonprofit organizations that inform adolescents about the danger of smoking. And red investors will consider investing in tobacco companies, as they have no reason to expect their returns to be poor in the future. In fact, if they believe the screening out of tobacco companies has reached a plateau, they will expect *higher* returns from them. Since these companies have access to a smaller supply of capital, they have to promise slightly higher returns to their investors, because their "cost of capital" has gone up. Some academic evidence confirms such a rise in the cost of capital of sin industry companies. For example, finance professors Harrison Hong and Marcin Kacperczyk of Princeton University have found that "sin stocks have higher expected returns than otherwise comparable stocks, consistent with them being neglected by norm-constrained investors."[6]

A sign that red investors might be taking an opposite view to that of yellow investors when it comes to broad industry exclusions is the appearance of the Vice Fund, among others. This mutual fund manages around $160 million, which it exclusively invests in "sin industries" like tobacco. As of November 2007, its largest holding, in which about 8% of its assets under management were invested, was the tobacco manufacturer Altria. The Vice Fund markets its product by stating on its website "that there are numerous investment opportunities in these [sin] sectors which have been largely overlooked by other funds." Over the last five years, it has returned an annualized 21.41%, beating most of its peers, and has benefited from strong coverage in the media, with headlines such as "Vice beats virtue in the battle for high returns."[7] Such a phenomenon is congruent with the view that red investors are not likely to join yellow or blue ones on a long-term, sustainable basis when it comes to industry exclusions: red investors anticipate that sooner or later, the quarantined sectors will have higher expected returns.

The example of tobacco screens shows how critical it is to assess the likelihood of change on an issue in order to perceive whether it is likely to succeed or to stagnate. Only if companies can make the demanded changes at reasonable costs will SRI go mainstream. As we have said, excluding entire industries is not the basis of sustainable SRI. Screening for feasible issues within each industry is.

Clearly, the cost of complying with the demands of responsible investors is an important determinant of whether a company will make a change or not. So SRI will either have an impact or be a protest in vain, depending on the realism of its demands.

Realistic change is more likely when issues are broken down into smaller possible changes that would be both more reasonable for a firm to satisfy and more likely to attract new investors. A not too distant analogy would be setting new speed limits. More citizens will favor decreasing the speed limit by 1 mph than by 10 mph, simply because all of those who favor a 10 mph decrease are automatically in favor of a 1 mph decrease, but not the other way around. For supporters of major change, a small increment is better than nothing and can encourage more, once new standards set in and new information arrives.

Breaking down issues into small changes will provide valuable momentum to the SRI movement. A large part of the movement is already operating in this spirit. For instance, a member of the advisory board of FTSE4Good, the index that serves as a benchmark for many European responsible investors, has affirmed: "The specific aim of FTSE4Good is to be demanding but achievable. As the average standard of good practice rises, so will the FTSE4Good bar rise."[8] In the scenario we envision for SRI, the demands investors make regarding a specific issue are such that a large majority of companies will fulfill them within the next five years.

▉▉▉▉　The Long Run

This notion of progressive change is also useful in thinking about the speed with which companies change. Many critics of SRI are skeptical because they feel that, despite the media attention to social responsibility, companies won't change overnight. Are they justified?

Consider the dot-com craze of the late 1990s. Yes, there was "irrational exuberance" around the dot-com phenomenon and the "new economy." But in hindsight, 10 years later, it is clear that the internet has indeed radically changed the way we work, communicate, travel, and consume. Between the believers and the doubters, if you were to pick a winner, whom would you pick? Do you think the naysayers were further from the mark than the new economy prophets? Are you judging them on the basis of their view of the future scope of the internet or their view of how long it will take the internet to achieve that scope?

SRI as an accelerator of change

We believe that the future scope of SRI is promising and exciting. And by emphasizing small changes, we are emphasizing that the impact of the SRI movement will be progressive rather than instantaneous. The speed at which this takes place will depend on other factors as well. Here's an example.

If governments signal that they will tighten regulations along the lines of the values that responsible investors fight for, the cost of compliance for companies will decrease, because by complying, companies are preparing for future standards: they are just choosing to pay the cost now rather than in a not so distant future. Doing so in advance might also save them the trouble of future litigation.

In chapter 4, we discussed how the SRI movement anticipated the development of environmental regulations and to some extent even provided impetus to them. These regulatory changes have accelerated SRI along this dimension, as companies taking environmental issues seriously have been performing well. So blue investors' concern about financial returns has decreased, and the interest of red investors has increased, accelerating participation in SRI.

The eventual outcome of regulatory discussions will depend on the outcome of the political game in several countries in the Americas, Europe, Asia, and Latin America. It is far from predictable. But ultimately, in democracies, regulations tend to reflect the social norms that prevail among citizens. When public outrage is high, politicians have to react. Consider this recent news report about worker safety standards in the steel industry:

> Dec. 10, 2007, Turin, Italy—Thousands of people marched Monday through the streets of Turin demanding improved workplace safety following the deaths of four workers in a factory fire in the north-western Italian city last week. The protestors numbered some 30,000 according to news reports, [and] included many metalworkers on an 8-hour work stoppage held in memory of their colleagues who died in the fire at the ThyssenKrupp steel-works plant.

Following this incident, Cesare Damiano, Italy's minister of labor, said in an interview in the Rome-based daily *La Republica* "that the centre-left government would press on with plans devised before Wednesday's blaze to make negligence in matters of workplace safety a crime punishable with the arrest of those responsible."[9] News coverage of this incident reflects its political ramifications:

> The accident triggered a huge emotional reaction in Italy. The speaker of Italy's lower house of parliament, Fausto

Bertinotti, urged a "major mobilization to fight work-related accidents," which he called a social scourge. Social Solidarity Minister Paolo Ferrero said the Italian employers' federation, Confindustria, should exclude companies that did not respect safety standards.[10]

This example illustrates the need for politicians to respond to public sentiment. It also suggests that SRI will have its fastest impact regarding those issues that arouse the strongest and broadest public sentiment—because they will be anticipating regulatory changes. Along these issues, SRI works as an *accelerator* of change. By convincing some companies to do better than the current regulation, it diminishes the force of industrial lobbies opposed to regulatory change and paves the way for government action responding to public demand.

In the very long run—a few decades—what will happen to the SRI movement? If almost all companies comply with the demands related to a specific issue, the battle for that issue is won. End of story. What comes next?

Here, again, it is important to be "value-specific." In some areas, pushing to the next level (using newer available technologies, for example) will still be a valid practice. As long as there is still room for improvement, there will be room for progress in that area, and it will be viable if enough investors support that progress. This scenario of the next incremental change will be likely if the previous change was only a partial fulfillment of the gap between companies' behavior and citizens' expectations. This scenario could also occur if social norms regarding a specific "value" become more demanding while the previous issue is getting resolved.

To go back to the case of workplace safety: Public intolerance for accidental death at work will likely keep getting stronger.

For example, Damanio said in an interview that "the number of job-related fatalities has decreased in Italy from an average of some 3,000 workers in the 1960s, to 1,400 in 2002 and 1,302 last year."[11] The improvement of safety at the workplace makes new accidents more, not less, shocking to the public. Because fatal accidents are rare, each of them has large media coverage and provokes public outrage. So for a value such as workplace safety, one can expect social norms to drift up, fueling new issues for SRI. Such issues will remain "young" for a long time, because standards will keep rising higher.

However, for some other issues, such continuous progress is not a likely scenario, simply because there will be no next step. For example, if carbon emissions fall below what is considered harmful for the environment, diminishing them further just won't constitute a valid cause any more. But it is likely that new issues will arise due to new social norms and new concerns. Changes in lifestyles and scientific discoveries might raise new concerns. For example, many more investors might become yellow with regard to an old "value." This mix of higher demands on older issues and on entirely new issues will keep the SRI movement busy.

▥ ■ ■   Returns on Investing in a "Sustainable Cause"

As noted, critics of the SRI movement often express doubts about its sustainability by speaking about returns. They agree that companies that do not respond positively to an issue will, in the long run, have higher returns (they have to promise higher returns when they raise capital). These irresponsible companies will attract all red and some blue investors to their capital, so the SRI movement will stop and plateau or maybe even contract back to the yellow core. Such critics point to the tobacco companies, for whom such evolution of returns has been documented (these companies now seem to provide relatively high returns). We agree. Tobacco exclusion is, as we discussed, not a sustainable SRI practice. We believe that such broad industry exclusions are not sustainable issues.

We do not think the same logic is applicable to sustainable issues. In the case of a sustainable issue, we see companies change in response to investors' demands, and eventually almost all (or a very large fraction of) companies end up complying with them after a few years. This totally changes the dynamics of stock returns. This is where the scenario the critics describe diverges from the one we anticipate.

To see this, keep in mind that as more firms comply, SRI around an issue will get stronger. This will then increase the cost of capital for the delinquent firms. And the cost to them of delinquency will keep increasing as more firms comply. Thus, in the case of a sustainable issue, the migration of all blue investors will leave ultimately very few—if any—delinquent firms.

These firms' total market capitalization will not be large enough to either cause large deviations in portfolio performance or to hold on to the red financial bounty hunters, who will now move on to another issue in anticipation of a similar migration of investors. In other words, the delinquent companies will eventually become a small, marginal economic phenomenon.

To reiterate: the example of screening out "sin" industries is misleading with regard to future returns; that is why these sectors still make up about 10% of the market. But a sustainable issue—defined narrowly—will yield incremental change over the long term, and the financial rewards will keep on coming.

Assuming an issue is indeed sustainable, in the sense we have defined, we can provide a broad estimate of the return differential between responsible and irresponsible firms along that issue during the transition. Assume that the complete migration of blue investors will take three to five years. After this period, all (but a few) firms will have changed, and hence there will be no difference between responsible and irresponsible firms. So the return difference between responsible and irresponsible firms along this cause will arise in the interim three- to five-year period.

If we assume that the fraction of capital grows from 10% to 50% in the five years due to the migration of many blue and red investors, on the basis of the numbers used in chapter 4, the cost of capital difference can be as high as 4%. As we have shown, a small difference in the cost of capital can result in a significant difference in firm value. In this case, this translates to a difference of up to 11% in firm value. This means that compared to companies that do not comply quickly with the cause, the market capitalization of those who do rises by an additional 11%. Dividing 11% by the number of years of the transition, say five, we get an average return differential of 2.2% per year in the five years. Surely, an overperformance of such magnitude is more than enough to attract the eye of RED investors.

We have focused in this chapter on the concept of a specific issue, as opposed to the broad notion of SRI. As a whole, SRI is a bundle of such specific issues, each with its own rate of progress and life cycle. As long as SRI manages to replenish its reservoir of sustainable issues, the transition performance we have just described will apply to SRI as a whole.

6

Your Values

Which issues are likely to bloom into sustainable ones and which ones will fade away? This chapter will give you a sense of what issues are feasible for an SRI portfolio. As you ponder the concerns you wish to express as an investor, your own personal set of issues will emerge. Some will be more important to you than others. With respect to some, you might be a yellow investor like Guy; with respect to others, you might be blue, like Kathy.

Can you have actual influence regarding all the issues you care about? We have already ruled out some for which SRI is not likely to be effective—those that corporations will find unrealistic to address. What issues are feasible? This is where your consciousness meets the practical world of finance.

Whether you achieve influence will depend on the nature of the issues you choose and whether they can be appropriately expressed in a portfolio.

On which specific issues, then—among the broad spectrum of those you care about—should you as an investor consider expressing your views? Let's start with identifying which of your issues are yellow and which are blue.

▮▮▮▮▮   ## Coloring Your Issues

We all have beliefs relating to different areas—religion, politics, food, money, and so on. There are many potential opinions. It is hardly surprising that some of them are not feasible for SRI. So let's get more specific. We suggest you write a list of 10 issues that matter to you—10 causes you wish to support.

For each, ask yourself "How important is it that I express this concern?" Assign scores of 0 for not important, 1 for somewhat important, and 2 for very important. Then ask yourself: "How important is it to me that my expression of this concern makes the world ascribe to it soon?" Score these in the same way. Enter your scores on a scorecard like the one shown in table 6.1 to help yourself clearly visualize your choices.

On the first question, a score of 0 implies that you should not express this particular issue through your SRI portfolio; a score of 2 suggests that you would be willing to bear a financial cost for doing so. After all, if you were not to express this value through your portfolio, you would probably do so by donating to an organization pursuing a related cause.

If your answer to the first question is not 0 but the answer to the second is 0, then your position on this issue is a matter of principle: You will incorporate this issue in your portfolio even if you know that doing so has no direct impact on the world. Do you feel "yellow" about any of the issues you have listed? Remember, this means you feel you *have to* avoid investing in all companies that are on the wrong side of this issue, because otherwise you would feel you were contributing to the problem. You will avoid investing in these companies even if there is a financial cost and even if there is no guarantee that doing so will change the world. (Add yellow to your scorecard for your yellow values.)

On the other hand, if the issue scores 1 or 2 in the second question, then you feel "blue" about it: you only want to express yourself

Table 6.1 Your Values Scorecard (Template).

Value	Desire to express?	Impact essential?	Color

through your portfolio on this issue only if you feel you can have an impact. (Add blue to your scorecard for your blue values.)

▪▪▪ The Two Feasibility Conditions

Once we have clarified our issues, we need to think of how to incorporate them in a portfolio. What conditions must the issues fulfill in order to be realistically and satisfactorily expressed in one's portfolio? We identify two; the first applies for both yellow and blue concerns, the second only for blue ones.

First, the issue must be such that one can reliably evaluate whether a firm is acting responsibly on it or not. Regardless of whether your feeling toward an issue is yellow or blue, answering this question about it must be the first step in incorporating it in an SRI portfolio.

If the answer cannot be determined, there will be no agreement among issues-conscious investors on which firms to exclude—to "punish"—or to reward for their performance on this issue. For the yellow investors, this will then strip away the moral clarity that is paramount.

It is therefore crucial to have a way to evaluate companies that obeys to a well-defined process and is as objective as possible. And it is important that companies not be able to "game the system."

No doubt, some would like to be viewed as responsible on an issue when in fact they are not. The process through which companies' performance is evaluated should make such gaming difficult. When we discuss social ratings later, we will examine on what responsibility issues it is currently possible to get such rigorous information.

Once you have classified an issue as yellow for you and it has passed this evaluation test, you should incorporate that issue in your portfolio.

For an issue you feel "blue" about, a second critical condition must be met: one must assess whether there is a large enough pool of investors with the same attitude. Because the power of SRI arises from collective action, the concerns of the rest of the investing population affect one's decision.

Only if enough investors share one's concern will companies make an effort to address it. Only then does it become worthwhile for you to express your concern for an issue through your portfolio. The issue needs to belong to a set that is widespread enough to have significant support and little opposition.

This condition eliminates issues purely driven by contentious religious beliefs and ideas based on controversial scientific evidence or any kind of eccentricity. Indeed, an issue that only a minority supports will not attract a sufficient pool of investors and is unlikely to become an issue companies need to care about. And if only a minority support an issue, chances are a large group is *against* it.

Blue investors must make sure the issues they choose to pursue fulfill both of the foregoing conditions. On both, we want to make sure we are not making our own subjective calls, for to do so would defeat our purpose. We want to let the data guide us to an objective assessment.

▮▮▮▮   Finding the Most Broadly Supported Issues

How does one determine what issues will be able to rally a large number of shareholders? Rather than using one's own introspection or common sense, which would leave the door open to one's subjectivity and biases, we propose a more objective process: directly analyzing how shareholders vote on different topics. The way to do this is to look at recent shareholder resolutions.

Every year, some responsible investors submit shareholder resolutions to directly challenge companies' behaviors. These resolutions are put on the ballot for the companies' shareholders' votes. Funds that submit resolutions to vote are often called "activists," as they try to directly induce change. In 2007, more than 1,150 shareholder resolutions were filed; of these, 331 were socially oriented. You can see all these resolutions on www.FundVotes.com (a nonprofit website that analyzes mutual fund and other large institutional investor voting records).

You can get a beginning sense of what issues are "investment relevant" by looking at the shareholder resolutions that have been filed in the previous year. These issues make up a good initial list of candidates for your "blue" SRI: any issue worth fighting for is likely to have been considered by SRI activists. (For the relevant issues reported by FundVotes.com for 2004–2006, see table 6.2.)

Note that none of these resolutions sounds very eccentric: We do not see any attempts to make companies endorse radically religious or political viewpoints. The socially active shareholders represented here know that such resolutions stand no chance of gathering sufficient support from the rest of the shareholder population. In fact, if a resolution is too eccentric, a company can ask the SEC for permission to omit it in the shareholder meeting.

To assess whether shareholder support for an issue is strong enough for our purposes, we need to determine a threshold: to set the bar. Proposals in their third year or more must score at least 10% to be resubmitted the next year. This number can work as our threshold; it is, in a sense, the bar shareholder resolutions have to pass to be "sustainable."

Table 6.3 shows the resolution issues that meet this criterion.

Table 6.2 A (Partial) List of the Current Responsibility Themes.

Theme of resolution	Specific issue	Average number of resolutions per year (2004–2006)
Environment	Environmental conservation	3
Environment	Environmental impact/reporting	5
Environment	Global warming/energy efficiency	9
Environment	Pay for social/environmental performance	3
Environment	Recycling	2
Environment	Efforts against nuclear risk/radioactive waste	3
Environment	Sustainability reporting	10
Environment	Operating forestry sustainability	2
Militarism	Stopping business with oppressive regimes	3
Militarism	Ethical criteria for military contracts and sales	7
Animal rights	Animal welfare/animal testing	14
Community	Charitable contributions	4
Community	Ethical lending	2
Customers	Against genetically engineered products	11
Customers	Higher access to drugs	5
Customers	Product safety	1
Customers	Against tobacco and cigarettes	9
Customers/ Environment	Fewer toxic chemicals	9
Employees	China labor standards	5
Employees	Human rights and workplace standards	15
Employees	Macbride Principles/Northern Ireland operations	6
Employees	Nondiscrimination and equal employment	11
Employees	Against offshoring	3
Employees	Reducing pay disparity	12
Employees	Higher retiree benefits	1
Employees	Vendor/contractor/supplier standards	4

Source: Author's computation based on data available at http://www.Fundvotes.com/.

As you can see, we end up with a relatively short list. Controversial topics such as "genetically engineered food" or "offshoring" are not on it. The issues are spread across the three broad core areas we have discussed earlier: protecting the environment; customers; and employees. These areas have a common feature: They are concerned with the stakeholders of firms (i.e., those directly affected by the decision of firms), as follows.

First, the *environment*. Firms can often ignore environmental standards in their attempts to grow, so they might pollute their surroundings. Many might suffer as a consequence—including people who live close to firms'

Table 6.3 Responsibility Themes with Significant Support.

Theme of resolution	Specific issue	Average percentage votes (2004–2006)
Environment	Environmental conservation	19%
Environment	Environmental impact/reporting	16%
Environment	Global warming/energy efficiency	15%
Environment	Sustainability reporting	22%
Customers	Higher access to drugs	13%
Customers/ Environment	Fewer toxic chemicals	10%
Employees	Human rights and workplace standards	16%
Employees	Macbride principles/Northern Ireland operations	12%
Employees	Nondiscrimination and equal employment	21%
Employees	Reducing pay disparity	11%
Employees	Higher retiree benefits	12%
Employees	Vendor/contractor/supplier standards	21%

Source: Author's computation based on data available at http://www.Fundvotes.com/.

production sites or future generations who might have to live in a polluted world and suffer the effects of erratic climate shifts.

Second, the *customers*. Firms can expose customers to health hazards through their products. In their desire to sell more, they might hide some critical information or advertise in a misleading way. Or a company that produces products that are critical to survival might not make them accessible to all—an example is the pricing of drugs in poor countries. Resolutions on these issues typically ask firms to raise their standards of product safety or remedy previously ignored situations that might pose a threat to customers.

Third, the *workers*. Firms' treatment of their workers might violate the basic tenets of internationally accepted human rights. In an attempt to save money, they might contract with suppliers who do the same. Resolutions on these issues typically ask that companies treat workers in compliance with human rights standards and provide them with benefits such as health insurance.

Reading resolutions' texts reveals that most use the argument that their adoption is likely to increase the firm's shareholder value and decrease the risks to which it is exposing itself. For example, the proposed resolution on China labor standards in Disney's January 2006 proxy statement states: "Human rights abuses in the overseas subsidiaries and suppliers of U.S. corporations can lead to negative publicity, public protests, and a loss of consumer confidence, which can have a negative impact on shareholder value."[1]

Thus, in your list of the issues you care about, you should keep in mind that those that can be presented as having an impact on future profits will have stronger resonance. That's because they will receive the votes of some red investors.

The issues we have identified—protecting the environment and caring for the needs of other human beings (customers and workers)—are widely agreed on by not only the U.S. but also the world population. They are broadly shared across countries with various cultures, religions, and economic status. Looking at the World Values Survey mentioned in chapter 1 confirms this: More than 68% of the 123,000 individuals surveyed declared that they "would give part of [their] income if certain that the money would be used to prevent environmental pollution." Asked what they thought a "just" society should provide, 71% declared it to be "very important" that "it guarantees basic needs for all." In addition, 45% agreed that "service to others is a very important aspect of life" and another 41% considered it "rather important."

Are Social Ratings Reliable?

As promised earlier, we will now explore how one goes about meeting the first condition for including a specific issue in one's SRI portfolio: one needs to be able to objectively evaluate whether or not a firm is acting responsibly on that issue. There is currently some debate about the reliability of the "social ratings" that are available for performing this evaluation. This concern has been a major source of skepticism about SRI. Challenging the objectivity of these ratings, some have claimed that they are based on subjective views of companies, are guided by public opinion, or are influenced by superficial corporate public relations activities. Firms that present a responsible façade are said to get preferential treatment even if they don't really change their behaviors. Some say these ratings do not treat all companies the same way, for example that a firm might be treated with more severity merely because it has a notorious past.

In a recent article, Henry Blodget, a former stock analyst, expressed the skepticism often encountered about social ratings:

> The methods for choosing good companies are still highly subjective. Screening criteria must be selected and ranked in terms of importance, and each company must be scored on dozens of complete attributes, often using imperfect or incomplete information.... The inherently subjective judgments, combined with the reality that most companies are sinful in some areas and saintly in others, lead some observers to call such rankings absurd.... Another challenge is that beauty might only be skin deep. As corporate social responsibility has gone mainstream, companies have spotted a juicy marketing and PR opportunity.[2]

Such criticism makes many potential investors shy away from SRI. They believe that trying to rank companies' social behaviors is like shooting in the dark. They suspect that social responsibility has become another marketing tool that large companies and their public relations people are exploiting to develop images of their behaviors that are far from reality.

The following exploration of how social ratings function these days will give you a sense of what you can expect from them and how you can use them to limit the scope of subjectivity when you evaluate whether or not a company is behaving responsibly.

The social ratings industry is still relatively young. The U.S. leader, KLD Analytics, started commercializing ratings in 1988. Today, several other companies also produce information for analyzing a company's social responsibility. Socially responsible funds can use this information to decide which companies satisfy their criteria. Such ratings companies include

Institutional Shareholders Services, a division of the RiskMetrics Group; Innovest Strategic Value Advisors; and Dow Jones Interactive. Several socially responsible funds, such as Calvert, also use their own research to select responsible companies. The Ethical Investment Research Service, the U.K. leader, was launched in 1983.

The contemporary social ratings industry is marked by increased competition. This is partly the result of red investors such as Ted— professional, profit-seeking ones who combine social ratings with their traditional analyses to produce high returns. These investors cannot be suspected of merely trying to "buy peace of mind." They are willing to pay a high price for precise, topical information; they are not interested in fuzzy information. This new demand has brought new players into the field, for example, Innovest, which was founded in 1995 with the mission of integrating sustainability and finance by identifying nontraditional sources of risk and value potential for investors. Innovest caters particularly to red investors: their website states that their clients view "extrafinancial" issues, "including environmental, social, and governance performance...as a potential source of risk or competitive advantage, not as a basis for moral judgments." Indirectly, red investors have played a role in improving the accuracy of social ratings.

In concert, companies have standardized their reports on social responsibility, following initiatives such as the Global Report Initiative. This is particularly true for environmental issues. In this field, quantitative data are available that make ratings objective and enable investors to compare companies within an industry. For example, in the United States, the Toxic Release Inventory maintained by the Environmental Protection Agency provides information on the toxic releases of all production facilities. This inventory was established under the Emergency Planning and Community Right-to-Know Act of 1986 and expanded by the Pollution Prevention Act of 1990. This information makes it possible to precisely measure a company's impact on the environment.[3]

What about information on, say, worker-related issues? It could be argued that such information is more "soft" in nature and therefore harder to evaluate without a subjective call. For such qualitative issues, can one define objective criteria? Can companies game the process?

To address these questions, we will use example of KLD's rating process as an example. The ratings KLD produces when it monitors firms' social responsibility form the basis of the Domini 400 Social Index, the first and largest socially screened index in the world. According to KLD, 15 of the top 25 institutional financial managers in the world use its research, and more than $10 billion is invested in funds on the basis of its ratings. The number of companies KLD tracks has expanded from around 500 to more than 3,000.

The KLD database consists of information about firm characteristics that have social and environmental impacts. These characteristics are used to assign measures of the company's good performance in terms of criteria that represent its "strengths" or its bad performance in terms of criteria that constitute "concerns." Each characteristic for which KLD screens is assigned a score of 0 or 1 and is part of an overall evaluation of a firm's social performance.

As a demonstration, consider the following example of the kind of information one can use from a ratings service to determine whether a company is responsible in a specific area. We call the screen shown here (the list of criteria used to judge the company on this issue) an "employee relationship screen"; we have put it together using some of the criteria that KLD provides in its "employee" category and some criteria that KLD labels differently (e.g., as "human rights" or "diversity").

Concerns

Union relations: The company has a history of notably poor union relations.

Health and safety: The company recently has either paid substantial fines or civil penalties for willful violations of employee health and safety standards.

Workforce reductions: The company has made significant reductions in its workforce in recent years.

Retirement benefits: The company has either a substantially underfunded defined benefit pension plan or an inadequate retirement benefits program.

Labor rights: The company's operations have had major recent controversies primarily related to labor standards in its supply chain.

Strengths

Union relations: The company has taken exceptional steps to treat its unionized workforce fairly.

Cash profit sharing: The company has a cash profit-sharing program through which it has recently made distributions to a majority of its workforce.

Employee involvement: The company strongly encourages worker involvement and/or ownership through stock options available to a majority of its employees, gain sharing, stock ownership, sharing of financial information, or participation in management decision making.

Retirement benefits: The company has a notably strong retirement benefits program.

Health and safety: The company has strong health and safety programs.

Work/life benefits: The company has outstanding employee benefits or other programs addressing work/life concerns, for example, childcare, elder care, or flextime.

Labor rights: The company has outstanding transparency
on overseas sourcing disclosure and monitoring, or has
particularly good union relations outside the United States,
or has undertaken labor rights–related initiatives that KLD
considers outstanding or innovative.

As you can see, this overall assessment of a company's
employee relations is based on a few simply defined indicators.
Some are indisputably objective—for example, the amount of
legal penalties the firm has paid. In any case, this is all information that cannot be easily manipulated by firms: they cannot
boast about a strong benefits program unless they actually offer
it to workers.

In the area of customer relations, an analysis similar to this
one can be constructed.

In the three areas of the environment, worker relations,
and customer relations, then, a firm's characteristics can be
described in a fairly objective way. There is not much room for
arbitrariness and gaming at this stage.

For "softer" screens, for example, in the area of human rights
in foreign countries (which we won't analyze in detail, as we
haven't labeled them as one of our three pillar issues), the
criteria are somewhat "softer." For example: "The company has
established relations with indigenous peoples near its proposed
or current operations (either in or outside the U.S.) that respect
the sovereignty, land, culture, human rights, and intellectual
property of indigenous peoples."

However, even in the case of such screens, firms that communicate positive information that does not match the facts expose
themselves to outrage in the media. In this age of blogs, gaps
between reality and official speeches rarely go undiscovered.
This is what happened recently to Gap Inc. after it represented
itself as having a strong program to control the work practices

of suppliers in poor countries. When a sweatshop was discovered in one of them, the company had no choice but to stick to its word, recalling all goods produced on that site and committing to tighter controls. Let us return to our three areas of concern: the environment, customers, and employees. We have shown that reliable information is available on specific aspects of a company's behaviors in these three areas. The next step is adding up the criteria the company does and does not meet in each of these three areas, and then combining the three totals to get a company's unique "social rating" (see fig. 6.1).

Note that if this procedure can be made transparent, the level of public confidence in social ratings can be increased. People do not like the idea of information being combined in a "black-box" way. Since they are not clear about the elements of the ratings, they doubt the company rankings. This feeling is summarized by *New York Times* columnist Joe Nocera in an article entitled "Well-Meaning but Misguided Stock Screens":

> I should concede right here that I've always harbored some suspicion about socially responsible investing.... My problem is that socially responsible investing oversimplifies the world, and in so doing distorts reality. It allows investors to believe that their money is only being invested in "good

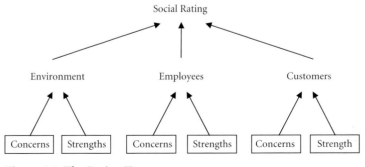

Figure 6.1 The Rating Tree.

companies," and they take foolish comfort in that belief. Rare is the company after all that is either all good or all bad. To put it another way, socially responsible investing creates the illusion that the world is black and white, when its real color is gray.[4]

The dilemma facing those who are developing the ratings is how to combine the various elements without creating any misleading distortions—in other words, how to represent the infinite spectrum of gray in a usable and truthful instrument. How much importance should one give to employee concerns vis-à-vis customer concerns? Should a firm that pays more attention to the environment than employees, say, be ranked above another firm that does the opposite? And within each area, should "strengths" and "concerns" be given equal importance? Should a firm that is neither good nor bad along environmental dimensions be rated the same way as one that takes exemplary steps to rectify an old "concern"?

The specific recipe KLD uses in developing firms' ratings is not public. The method employed by many academic studies of the same issues, however, is known. The studies add up "strengths" and subtract "concerns" to get, say, an environmental rating for a company—a rather arbitrary way to solve these dilemmas.

Such arbitrary procedures implicitly are tantamount to assigning levels of importance to a company's behavior characteristics. We feel the rater should not make these decisions, because they should depend on each individual's own preferences. What the rater should (and often does) provide is an accurate description of the characteristics of companies. Ideally, once this is done, the investor, not the rating agency, is the judge. But this is easier said than done. For example, showing how complicated this exercise could be, even with a highly simplified framework of only three criteria ("strengths" or "concerns") in three areas of concern (environment, customers, employees), there are 262,144 different ways a company can appear.

░░▓▓■ Tailoring Your Portfolio

Our goal is to give you, the investor, the power to decide how to combine the various ratings of companies' "concerns" and "strengths" without making the process too cumbersome. We believe that the method we will present here for classifying firms in various responsibility areas both is simple and solves the rater's dilemma.

Using this method, you can tailor a portfolio for yourself that both suits your subjective attitudes, is practically feasible.

Let us start with your chosen blue issues.

Let's say we have constructed a portfolio for each of our three issue areas. You can now choose a mix of them that best expresses your priorities. We have made each one a "zero-concern" portfolio; for example, "Environment Zero-Concern" is an industry-balanced portfolio of firms that belong to the S & P 500 and have no "concerns" in the environment area. Similarly, "Customers Zero-Concern" and "Employees Zero-Concern" are industry-balanced portfolios of firms that belong to the S & P 500 and have no "concerns" in these areas.

You might want more than this "minimum standard": You might want to express stronger support for firms that set the bar higher.—that reach out to the next frontier in your chosen area. In that case, you want to reward "strengths" and not just the absence of "concerns." So that you can express this stronger preference, let's say we have also constructed for each of the

three areas an industry-balanced portfolio of S & P 500 companies that not only have zero "concerns" but also have at least
one "strength." We call these three portfolios "Environment
Zero-Concern Plus," "Employees Zero-Concern Plus," and
"Customers Zero-Concern Plus."

The Plus portfolios are subsets of the "zero-concern" firms,
because they are selected from among them. This makes the
Zero-Concern Plus portfolios less diversified and therefore
potentially more volatile. Comparing their past performances
to that of the Zero-Concern ones can give you a sense of their
financial attractiveness. When we compared the average monthly
return and monthly volatility (a measure of risk) over 1999–
2007 for these two, as expected, we found that the addition of
the one "strength" to make the Plus portfolio increases risk—
and, it turns out, reduces average returns as well. Historically,
there is a financial cost to this add-on. However, if you believe
that in the future the companies that have the added "strength"
will outperform their peers who do not have it, investing in a
Plus portfolio is a way to act on that view.

How should you allocate your money between these different
portfolios?

Table 6.4 Financial Performance (1999–2007).

Portfolio	Monthly return	Monthly volatility	Number of firms
S & P 500	0.40%	3.92%	500
Environment Zero-Concern	0.52%	4.08%	355
Environment Zero-Concern Plus	0.45%	4.10%	35
Employees Zero-Concern	0.49%	3.94%	370
Employees Zero-Concern Plus	0.48%	4.05%	180
Customers Zero-Concern	0.46%	4.10%	315
Customers Zero-Concern Plus	0.37%	4.43%	40

Table 6.5 Your Areas Scorecard (Template).

Area	Desire to express?	Impact essential?	Color
Environment			
Employees			
Customers			

First, let us go back to the 10 issues you listed earlier. Determine which ones fit, broadly speaking, into the areas of environment, employees, or customers. For each area, as you did earlier (at the beginning of this chapter) for each of your 10 important values, ask yourself how important it is to you that you express it, and assign scores of 0 for not important, 1 for somewhat important, and 2 for very important. Then, again as you did earlier, ask yourself how important it is to you that your expression of this concern makes the world subscribe to it soon, and score these answers in the same way.

Fill in your scores on the scorecard shown in table 6.5. (Note that it is the same as table 6.1, except that the three issue areas are listed in the left column. If more than one of your 10 listed concerns fall in one of our 3 broad issues, you can compute an average of their scores for that corresponding broad issue.) Now add to the scorecard your color for each of the broad issues, as you did on the earlier one. This your feasible "SRI card." Remember that if you are a yellow investor regarding an issue, your "impact score" will be 0, as in this area you will feel compelled to invest responsibly with little regard to impact.

Now, let's tailor an imaginary portfolio for you to demonstrate how it can be done. We'll assume that out of your original 10 issues, 7 did not fit our three areas, and each of the remaining 3 fit one of them. You feel "blue" on all three.

Table 6.6 Prepare Your Portfolio (Template).

Area	Option	Selection	Fraction in total portfolio
Environment	Zero-Concern		
	Zero-Concern Plus		
Employees	Zero-Concern		
	Zero-Concern Plus		
Customers	Zero-Concern		
	Zero-Concern Plus		

The first step is to complete the two blank columns on the right side of table 6.6.

In the "Selection" column, for each area, you will be selecting an option that reflects how important it is to you to express your views in that area. Use your scores. If your desire to express in an area is between 0 and 1 (somewhat important), enter a check mark to indicate that you choose the Zero-Concern option. If your score is between 1 and 2 (very important), select the Zero-Concern Plus option in that area. If your score is 0 (not important), do not select any option in that area—leave it blank.

Next, in the "Fraction of Total Portfolio" column, for each area, you will enter a percentage that reflects how important it is to you that your expression of this concern makes the world subscribe to it soon. Again, use your scores on this question. For each area where you have entered a check mark, enter a percentage that reflects your score, as follows:

If your score is the same in all three areas, each should be assigned 33.3%.

If your score is the same in two areas and 0 in the third area, each of the two should be 50%.

If your score in one area is 2 (very important), your score in a second area is 1 (somewhat important), and your score in

the third area is 0 (not important), then the first area should
be 66.6%, and the second area should be 33.3%.
If your score is 1 in two areas and 2 in the third area, the first two
should each be 25%, and the third should be 50%.
If your score is 2 in two areas and 1 in the third area, the first two
should each be 40%, and the third should be 20%.

The rationale behind this procedure is simple. The Zero-
Concern-Plus option will signal your view more loudly and
effectively but is also financially less attractive. So you should
only choose that option for an area where it is very important to
you to express your view. And the percentages express the reality
that if you want to have impact in an area, you must invest more
in it; thus, it makes sense for the amount you invest to corre-
spond to the degree to which you want that impact.

An advantage of the procedure we have presented here is
that it combines different issue areas in a transparent way and
relies on your own preferences to do so. A frequent criticism
of SRI funds is that the managers of these funds have to pick
their own rules to decide what to do regarding a company
that does well in one area but not in others, not necessarily
reflecting their client's priorities for different issues. "Most
large SRI firms...[have] choices [that] vary so much that
what they do is less about 'socially responsible investing' than
about their manager's personal preferences," Blodget writes.[5]
Investors are often suspicious about the fact that the large
SRI funds do not clarify exactly why they have the different
holdings they have: "Among the 50 largest stocks, 40% trigger
a split decision [i.e. different choices of whether to invest or
not] among the Vanguard Calvert Fund, Domini Social Equity
Fund and the Citizens Index Fund. The social investing fund
firms aren't always forthcoming about why companies don't
make their lists and their funds. At Calvert, they have a policy

that they don't speak about companies that fail on a social screen."[6]

The procedure we have described is somewhat immune to this problem. You can choose a mix of options that express your views on different well-defined issues rather than having to choose one option that represents several issues at once. This procedure is adapted for investors who feel "blue" about our three core issue areas. They need not be worried that a company that shows up in, say, the environment options does not show up in, say, the customer options. How much impact these investors' expressions of their views have, after all, depends on how much money they put into investments that reflect these views. Our procedure, then, differs from the more orthodox "0 or 1"— or "black or white"—screening procedure.

■■■■ **Kathy's and Guy's Portfolios**

To illustrate more concretely how our method works and what impact it has on financial performance, we'll take a look at the portfolios that Kathy and Guy might pick. Let's say that Kathy's scorecard looks like the one shown in table 6.7.

The procedure we propose will lead from this scorecard to the portfolio shown in table 6.8.

What can we tell Kathy about the risks of this portfolio? Historically—in the period 1999–2007—her portfolio would

Table 6.7 Kathy's Areas Scorecard.

Area	Desire to express?	Impact essential?	Color
Environment	1	2	
Employees	2	2	
Customers	1	2	

Table 6.8 Kathy's Portfolio.

Category	Option	Selected?	Fraction in portfolio
Environment	Zero-Concern	X	33.3%
	Zero-Concern Plus		
Employees	Zero-Concern		
	Zero-Concern Plus	X	33.3%
Customers	Zero-Concern	X	33.3%
	Zero-Concern Plus		

Table 6.9 Kathy's Portfolio Performance, 1999–2007.

Portfolio	Monthly return	Monthly volatility
S & P 500	0.40%	3.92%
Kathy's	0.49%	4.02%

not have been significantly more risky than the S & P 500 and would have had slightly higher returns.

Her portfolio did not underperform compared to the S & P 500 during the 2001 stock-market decline. On the basis of historical performance, for a given month, there is a less than 5% likelihood that Kathy's portfolio will have a return inferior to the S & P 500 by more than 1% (see fig. 6.2).

Through this portfolio, Kathy can voice a well-defined message about her values. She can "vote" for what she believes would be a better world and for her priorities for change. Joined with the collective surge of the SRI movement, her voice will have an impact, and it will have a negligible financial cost to her, if any.

Kathy's preferences led to all her issues being classified as blue. But if you have even one yellow area, it affects the other two areas in your portfolio as well. For example, if you are yellow on the environment—a score of 2 on desire to express and a score

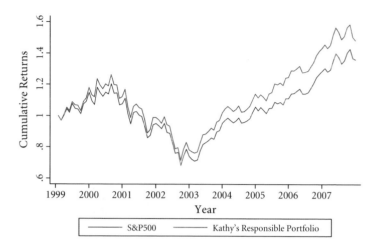

Figure 6.2 Kathy's Responsible Portfolio vs. S & P 500 (Cumulative Returns).

of 0 on the desire to have impact—it won't be acceptable for you to simply choose the Employment-Zero-Concern option, as it might contain some companies that have environmental "concerns." As Nocera has rightly pointed out, firms are not all good or bad; they are both. So if you have a yellow area, you need to make sure to exclude from the other areas any firms that have "concerns" in your yellow area. In fact, any company that is not compatible with one of your "yellow" issues (even an issue outside the three we have described as feasible for blue investors, such as tobacco) would have to be excluded from your portfolio.

Guy's portfolio demonstrates how one must take yellow issues into account. Guy feels "yellow" not only about being a voice for change in our three core issue areas (environment, employees, and customers) but also about opposing tobacco, weapons, and gambling companies—as mentioned in chapter 3. The most diversified portfolio we can create for Guy is one that invests in companies that have zero "concerns" in all three core

Table 6.10 Guy's Portfolio Performance (1999–2007).

Portfolio	Monthly return	Monthly volatility
S & P 500	0.40%	3.92%
Guy's	0.51%	4.37%

areas and are also not involved in the industries he rejects. To make Guy's portfolio as diversified as possible, for the industries that are present in it, we will invest in them proportionally to their importance in the S & P 500. As one might expect, Guy's portfolio has more risk than Kathy's—even though Kathy uses a Zero-Concern-Plus option in the employees area and Guy uses only Zero-Concern options across all areas. So Guy's portfolio only contains about 100 companies, but this is fine with him. He is willing to sacrifice diversification for the sake of having a portfolio that excludes companies that are incompatible with his values.

The Limitations and the Promise

An SRI portfolio can be tailored to fit your personal desires. However, it cannot reflect the whole spectrum of your opinions and values, because corporations' levels of responsibility on some issues cannot be reliably measured, and this fact rules them out for both yellow and blue investors. In addition, some other issues are not of interest to a large enough population for investing to have an impact, thus ruling them out for blue investors. This restricts the set of issues about which an SRI investor can meaningfully express his or her views. We believe that the three areas of the environment, employee relations, and customers' safety are the pillars of a blue SRI portfolio, because these areas are cared about by a majority and because firms' performance in these areas can be measured in a relatively objective way.

What We Believe

Behind the many myths and mysteries of investment management lies a simple fact: investing in who you are is possible (chapter 1). Several firms that rate companies and several funds that manage SRI portfolios make this possible. And SRI appears to be a growing phenomenon. With increased public moneys in equity markets, SRI is getting more attention. And several other factors (chapter 4) are combining to bring SRI from the fringes into the mainstream of the investment management industry.

Can SRI provide competitive returns? Can it change the world? Yes and yes, if you incorporate sustainable issues in your portfolio and you do so in a way that does not sacrifice diversification. As we have shown, investors' action on issues that are sustainable—that companies can act on at a reasonable cost (chapter 5)—will cause changes in corporate behavior. We have given several examples of this (chapter 2). And sustainable issues can be incorporated into your portfolio without hurting its financial performance. In chapter 3 we discussed the risks you should be wary of. And as we saw in chapter 4, a case could even be made for SRI portfolios' superior financial performance.

All this leads us to believe that, in some basic and important areas, SRI will have a positive impact on both your portfolio and the world around you. Your money can be put to work for a dual purpose: changing the world and building your financial wealth.

APPENDIX

The following companies offer (one or more) socially responsible funds. This list is based on data from www.socialinvest.org.

Equity/Balanced Funds

Legg Mason Investment Counsel
Walden Asset Management
The Appleseed Fund
Calvert
Citizens Advisers
Domini Social Investments
Dover Responsibility Fund
Integrity Growth and Income Fund
Mennonite Mutual Aid (MMA)—MMA Praxis Mutual Funds
Green Century Funds
Neuberger Berman
Portfolio 21
Parnassus Investments
Socially Responsible Utilities Fund
Pax Funds
New Alternatives Fund, Inc.
Sierra Club Mutual Funds

GAMCO Asset Management, Inc.
TIAA-CREF
Walden Asset Management
Winslow Green Growth Fund

Bond (Fixed Income Funds)

Access Capital Strategies, LLC
Calvert
Citizens Advisers
Domini Social Investments
Parnassus Investments
Pax Funds
Mennonite Mutual Aid (MMA)—MMA Praxis Mutual Funds
Community Capital Management

NOTES

Introduction

1. This figure is based on the assets under management with the signatories of the UN Principles for Responsible Investment.

Chapter 1

1. Dan McDougall, "Child Sweatshop Shame Threatens Gap's Ethical Image," *Observer*, October 28, 2007.
2. Ying Lou and Winnie Zhu, "PetroChina Feels Sudan Heat as Fidelity Sells Shares," *International Herald Tribune*, May 16, 2007.
3. Jeremy Pelofsky, "Bush Signs into Law Sudan Divestment Measure," Reuters, January 1, 2008.
4. United Nations, *Report of the International Commission of Inquiry on Darfur to the United Nations Secretary-General (Pursuant to Security Council Resolution 1564 of 18 September 2004)*, January 2005, www.un.org/news/dh/sudan/com_inq_darfur.pdf.
5. *The Cultural Creatives: How 50 Million People Are Changing the World* (New York: Harmony Books, 2000).
6. See Vernon Henderson, "Effects of Air Quality Regulations," *American Economic Review* 86 (September 1996): 789–813.
7. M. Greenstone, "The Impacts of Environmental Regulations on Industrial Activity: Evidence from the 1970 and 1977 Clean Air Act Amendments and the Census of Manufactures," *Journal of Political Economy* 110 (2002): 1175–1219. Counties that had levels of pollution concentrations exceeding the federal standards of the Clean Air Act had to force companies to decrease their releases of pollutant chemicals.
8. R. Jeffrey Smith and Jeffrey H. Burnham, "Drug Bill Demonstrates Lobby's Pull, Democrats Feared Industry Would Stall Bigger Changes," *Washington Post*, January 12, 2007.

9. Quoted in M. Statman, *Socially Responsible Investors and Their Advisors*, working paper, Santa Clara University, June 2007.

10. "India's Rich Getting Richer," *Financial Express*, online ed., September 22, 2006; *Inside the Affluent Space: Changing Lifestyle Expectations of the Affluent in India, American Express Report*, September 2006.

11. R. Inglehart, M. Basanez, J. Diez-Medrano, L. Halman, and R. Luijkx, eds., *Human Beliefs and Values* (Mexico: Siglo XXI Editores, 2004), 8.

12. R. Inglehart and C. Welzel, *Modernization, Cultural Change, and Democracy* (Cambridge: Cambridge University Press, 2005), 52.

13. Ibid., 52.

14. Our own multivariate analysis, based on the World Value Survey data, publically available at http://www.worldvaluessurvey.org/.

15. We find that when per capita gross domestic product is 30% smaller, the more highly educated are 1% more likely to strongly support helping the environment.

16. Shaohua Chen and Martin Ravallion, *Absolute Poverty Measures for the Developing World, 1981–2004*, Development Research Group, working paper, World Bank, March 2007, http://www-wds.worldbank .org/servlet/WDSContentServer/WDSP/IB/2007/04/16/000016406_ 20070416104010/Rendered/PDF/wps4211.pdf.

17. James Davies, Susanna Sandstrom, Anthony Shorrocks, and Edward Wolf, *The World Distribution of Household Wealth*, World Institute for Development Economics Research, working paper (http://www.iariw .org/papers/2006/davies.pdf), December 2006.

18. Thomas Piketty, "Income Inequality in the United States, 1913–1998," *Quarterly Journal of Economics* 118 (1) (2003): 1–39.

19. Noelle Barton and Ian Wilhelm, "Foundation Assets Grow Sharply: Many Funds Expect to Give More in 2007, Chronicle Survey Finds," *Chronicle of Philanthropy*, April 5, 2007, p. 1, http://www.philanthropy .com/free/articles/v19/i12/12000701.htm.

20. Russell Sparkes, *Socially Responsible Investment: A Global Revolution* (Chichester: Wiley, 2002), 53.

21. John C. Harrington, *Investing with Your Conscience* (New York: Wiley, 1992), 34.

22. Ibid., 34.

23. Ibid., 27.

24. http://www.tiaa-cref.org/about/press/about_us/releases/ pressrelease208.html, July 10, 2007, Press Release, TIAA-CREF.

25. "Defined Contribution Plans and Socially Responsible Investing," *Social Investment Forum*, June 2007, http://www.socialinvest.org/pdf/ research/DC%20Plans%20and%20SRI%20in%20US.pdf.

26. *Facts from EBRI*, Employee Benefit Research Institute, Washington, D.C., June 2007.
27. European SRI mutual fund assets jump 43%, Hugh Wheelan, November 1, 2007, www.responsible-investor.com/beta/article/ european_sri_mutual_fund_assets_jump_43/.
28. Statutory Instrument 1999 no. 1849; Amendment Regulations 1999, http://www.opsi.gov.uk/si/si1999/19991849.htm.
29. Advisory Opinion Letter to Calvert's General Counsel, Department of Labor, May 28, 1998, http://www.calvert.com/pdf/sri_dol_letter.pdf.
30. Mark Landler, "Norway Keeps Nest Egg from Some US Companies," *New York Times*, May 4, 2007.

Chapter 2

1. Bengt Holmström and Steve Kaplan, "The State of U.S. Corporate Governance: What's Right and What's Wrong?" *Journal of Applied Corporate Finance* 15–3 (spring 2003): 8–20.
2. See, for example, the Gompers-Ishii-Metrick index, produced by the Investor Responsibility Research Center.
3. Diane Del Guercio, Laura Wallis, and Tracie Woidtke, *Do Boards Pay Attention When Institutional Investors "Just Vote No"?* working paper, University of Oregon, September 2006.
4. The potential conflicts of interest are twofold: Investment banks have companies as clients for corporate issuance and merger-and-acquisition business. Mutual funds also have companies as clients as they compete to be 401(k) plan providers.
5. Securities Exchange Commission, *Final Rule: Proxy Voting by Investment Advisers*, release no. IA-2106; file no. S7-38-02, www.sec .gov/rules/final/ia-2106.htm.
6. W. T. Carleton, J. M. Nelson, and M. S. Weisbach, "The Influence of Institutions on Corporate Governance through Private Negotiations: Evidence from TIAACREF," *Journal of Finance* 53, 4 (1998): 1335–1362.
7. *Socially Responsible Investing at TIAA-CREF, 2006–2007 Update*, www.tiaa-cref.org/about/press/about_us/releases/pdf/TIA_615_SRI-Update_v07.pdf.
8. Support for management and shareholder-sponsored resolutions by fund families in 2007, www.fundvotes.com.
9. Robert Heinkel, Alan Kraus, and Josef Zechner, "The Effect of Green Investment on Corporate Behavior," *Journal of Financial and Quantitative Analysis* 36, 4 (December 2001): 431. See also

Amir Barnea, Robert Heinkel, and Alan Kraus, *Corporate Social Responsibility*, working paper, University of British Columbia, 2004.

10. Harrison Hong and Marcin Kacperczyk, *The Price of Sin*, working paper, Princeton University, 2006.

11. Leonardo Becchetti, Rocco Ciciretti, and Iftekhar Hasan, *Corporate Social Responsibility and Shareholder's Value: An Event Study Analysis*, working paper no. 2007–6, Federal Reserve Bank of Atlanta, April 2007.

12. See, for example, Andrei Shleifer and Robert W. Vishny, "Equilibrium Short Horizons of Investors and Firms," *American Economic Review* 80(2).

13. Natasha Burns, Simi Kedia, and Marc L. Lipson, "The Effects of Institutional Ownership and Monitoring: Evidence from Financial Restatements," January 2006, available at, http://ssrn.com/abstract=880788.

14. Edith Hotchkiss and Deon Strickland, "Does Shareholder Composition Matter? Evidence from the Market Reaction to Corporate Earnings Announcements," *Journal of Finance* 58 (August 2003): 1469–98.

15. http://www.sec.gov/Archives/edgar/data/1288776/000119312504142742/ds1a.htm (S-1 registration statement).

16. José-Miguel Gaspar, Massimo Massa, and Pedro Matos, "Shareholder Investment Horizon and the Market for Corporate Control," *Journal of Financial Economics* 76, 1 (April 2005): 135–65.

17. "Report on Responsible Investing Trends in the U.S. 2001," *Social Investment Forumt*, 2001, http://www.socialinvest.org/pdf/research/Trends/2001%20Trends%20Report.pdf.

18. Nicolas Bollen, "Mutual Fund Attributes and Investor Behavior," *Journal of Financial and Quantitative Analysis*, forthcoming.

19. Available at www.regjeringen.no/en/dep/fin/Selected-topics/andre/Ethical-Guidelines-for-the-Government-Pension-Fund-Global-/Recommendations-and-Letters-from-the-Advisory-Council-on-Ethics/Recommendation-of-15-November-2005.html?id=450120.

20. Heather Dale, "Green Plea from US Funds," *Global Pensions*, November 16, 2007, available at http://globalpensions.com.

Chapter 3

1. "*Defined Contribution Plans and Socially Responsible Investing in the United States*, Mercer Report for Social Investment Forum. Mercer Investment Consulting is a leading global provider of investment consulting services and offers customized guidance at every stage of the investment decision, risk management, and investment monitoring

process. Mercer Investment Consulting's Responsible Investment business helps investment fiduciaries integrate environmental, social, and corporate governance (ESG) considerations into investment decision making and ownership practices. Mercer Investment Consulting is a unit of Mercer Human Resource Consulting, an operating company of Marsh & McLennan Companies, Inc. (MMC). MMC lists its stock (ticker symbol: MMC) on the New York, Chicago, and London stock exchanges. The research was undertaken with project partners AltruShare Securities, Calvert, FTSE Group, Neuberger Berman, Northern Trust, and TIAA-CREF.

2. Quoted in a Socialinvest press release about the report cited in note 1, June 5, 2007, www.socialinvest.org/news/releases/pressrelease .cfm?id=48.

3. The contribution for which Harry Markowitz received the 1990 Nobel Prize in economics was first published in his essay "Portfolio Selection" (1952) and in his book *Portfolio Selection: Efficient Diversification* (1959). He developed in this work a theory for optimal investment of wealth in assets that differ in regard to their expected returns and risks. William Sharpe was awarded the Nobel Prize for his achievements in asset pricing, leading to the "capital asset pricing" formula, work that can be found in his essay "Capital Asset Prices: A Theory of Market Equilibrium under Conditions of Risk" (1964).

4. Harrison Hong and Marcin Kacperczyk, *The Price of Sin*, working paper, Princeton University, 2006.

5. Report on CalsTRS Meeting by the California Retired Teachers Association, April 2008, found at http://www.crta5.org/calstrsapr.pdf.

6. Christopher Geczy, Robert Stambauh, and David Levin, *Investing in Socially Responsible Mutual Funds*, working paper, Wharton School, 2005.

7. S. Hamilton, H. Jo, and M. Statman, "Doing Well While Doing Good? The Investment Performance of Socially Responsible Mutual Funds," *Financial Analysts Journal* (November/December 1993): 62–66.

8. Here is how we proceeded. We used only "industry-agnostic" "concerns" from KLD—that is, we did not base our selection on KLD "concerns" that would eliminate all companies of a given industry. For example, we did not keep "the company derives substantial revenues from the sale of coal or oil" (which would eliminate the entire oil industry) as a "concern," but we kept "concerns" about the levels of companies' "liabilities for hazardous waste" or "emissions of toxic chemicals," as these are "concerns" that touch some industries more than others but not all companies in an industry.

9. The beta of the responsible portfolio is 1.

10. Marc Lane Investment Management, Inc., *Corporate Behavioral Screening: A New Perspective for Social Investors*, 2004.
11. John G. Simon, Charles W. Powers, and Jon P. Gunnemann, *The Ethical Investor: Universities and Corporate Responsibility* (New Haven, CT: Yale University Press, 1972). This book established criteria and procedures a university could follow in responding to requests from members of its community to consider factors in addition to economic return when making investment decisions and exercising its rights as a shareholder. The book is now in the public domain and is available at http://acir .yale.edu/.
12. Ibid., 12.

Chapter 4

1. Quoted from the United Nations, Principles of Responsible Investing's website at www.unpri.org/about/.
2. Aaron K. Chatterji, David Levine, and Michael Toffel, *How Well Do Social Ratings Actually Measure Corporate Social Responsibility?* working paper, Duke University, 2007.
3. Michael Harrison, "Mittal Charm Offensive Fails to Halt Flak over Pounds 13 Billion Arcelor," *Independent*, January 31, 2006.
4. Interview with Lakshmi Mittal, *Les Echos*, January 30, 2006.
5. "Mittal, the Natural Alliance," Brochure published by Mittal and filed by the company with the U.S. Securities and Exchange Commission on May 19, 2006, available at www.secinfo.com/d14D5a.v3Hcv.c.htm.
6. Nicolas Véron, "M. Mittal peut-il dédramatiser la mondialisation?" *La Tribune*, February 13, 2006.
7. Economists call this an "endogeneity problem."
8. "Corporate Responsibility: Burden or Opportunity," *Grant Thornton's Survey of U.S. Business Leaders*, 15th ed. (2007).
9. Ibid., 62.
10. Michael E. Porter and Forest L. Reinhardt, "A Strategic Approach to Climate," *Harvard Business Review* 85, 10 (October 2007): 22–26.
11. Quoted from company presentation on Innovest's website at http:// www.innovestgroup.com.
12. "Introducing GS Sustain," Report published by Goldman Sachs, June 22, 2007, available at http://www.unglobalcompact.org/docs/ summit2007/gs_esg_embargoed_until030707pdf.pdf.
13. "Collision course. New European rules are bad news for Germany's car makers," Munich and Stuttgart, *Economist* 385, 8560 (December 22, 2007): 105–6, available at http://www.economist.com/business/ displaystory.cfm?story_id=10329196).

14. Ibid.

15. Jeroen Derwall, Nadja Guenster, Rob Bauer, and Kees Koedijk, "The Eco-Efficiency Premium Puzzle," *Financial Analysts Journal* 61 (March–April 2005): 51–63.

16. Alex Edmans, *Does the Stock Market Fully Value Intangibles? Employee Satisfaction and Equity Prices*, working paper, Wharton School, October 2007.

17. Technichally, this is the alpha of the portfolio over the Carhart four-factor model. Concretely, this means that this is the component of the portfolio's return which cannot be explained as a reward for risk.

18. We also tried to apply industry exclusions to this portfolio. We excluded companies from our "superresponsible" portfolio that do business in tobacco, alcohol, gaming, or weapons, and investigated the returns of the resulting portfolio. While this smaller set of stocks has a marginally less impressive performance, they do not underperform the rest of the S & P 500 stocks. So, perhaps, the overperformance of superresponsible companies is strong enough to cover the loss of diversification that comes with excluding industries and a large number of companies. In that case, even someone like Guy who is unwilling to invest in "sin industries" does not have to sacrifice as much as he did when screens were purely negative and excluded entire industries.

    Even a combination of industry-agnostic screens and industry exclusions is not too costly.

19. Eugene Fama, "The Behavior of Stock Market Prices," *Journal of Business* 38, 1 (January 1965): 34–105.

20. Andrei Shleifer and Robert W. Vishny, "The Limits of Arbitrage," *Journal of Finance* 52, 1 (March 1997): 35–55.

21. Malcolm Baker and Jeff Wurgler, "Investor Sentiment in the Stock Market," *Journal of Economic Perspectives*, forthcoming.

22. Robert Heinkel, Alan Kraus, and Josef Zechner, "The Effect of Green Investment on Corporate Behavior," *Journal of Financial and Quantitative Analysis* 36, 4 (December 2001): 431 and 440–41, figs. 1 and 2.

23. Assuming a growth rate of 2%, the price-to-earning ratio using the Gordon formula, $V/E = 1/(r - g)$, changes from 12.5 to 13.9.

24. W. Edwards, "Conservatism in Human Information Processing," in B. Kleinmutz, ed., *Formal Representation of Human Judgment* (New York: Wiley, 1968), 17.

25. Nicholas Barberis, Andrei Shleifer, and Robert Vishny, "A Model of Investor Sentiment," *Journal of Financial Economics* 49, 3 (September 1998): 307–43.

26. "DC Plans and SRI," *Social Investment Forum*, June 2007, p. 8.

27. Ray Fisman, Geoffrey Heal, and Vinay B. Nair, "A Model of Corporate Philanthropy," Columbia University working paper, 2006.

28. Dawn Cowie, "Demand Is High for Renewable-Energy IPOs," *Wall Street Journal*, November 8, 2007.

29. J. G. Gimpel and J. E. Schuknecht, "Political Participation and the Accessibility the Ballot Box," *Political Geography* 22 (2003): 471–88.

30. David Vogel, *The Market for Virtue*, Washington: Brookings Press, 2005), 68.

31. Mike Foster, "Getting Emissions on the Books," *Wall Street Journal*, November 6, 2007.

32. Ibid.

33. Quoted on Global Reporting Initiative's website at http://www .globalreporting.org/NewsEventsPress/.

34. Esther Duflo and Emmanuel Saez, "The Role of Information and Social Interactions in Retirement Plan Decisions: Evidence from a Randomized Experiment," *Quarterly Journal of Economics* 118 (2003): 815–42.

35. M. Massa and A. Simonov, *History versus Geography: The Role of College Interaction in Portfolio Choice*, working paper, Centre for Economic Policy Research, London, 2005.

36. Steve Schueth, "Socially Responsible Investing in the United States," *Journal of Business Ethics* 43 (March 2003): 3.

37. Esther Duflo, "Grandmothers and Granddaughters: Old-Age Pensions and Intrahousehold Allocation in South Africa," *World Bank Economic Review* 17, 1 (2003): 1–25.

Chapter 5

1. Michael J. Cooper, Orlin Dimitrov, and P. Raghavendra Rau, "A Rose .com by Any Other Name," *Journal of Finance* 56, 6 (2001): 2371–88.

2. P. Raghavendra Rau, Ajay Patel, Igor Osobov, Ajay Khorana, and Michael J. Cooper, "Managerial Actions in Response to a Market Downturn: Valuation Effects of Name Changes in the Dot.com Decline," *Journal of Corporate Finance* 11, 1–2 (2005): 319–35.

3. Jose Scheinkman, "Social Interactions," in *The New Palgrave Dictionary of Economics*, 2nd ed. (Palgrave: Macmillan, May 27, 2008).

4. R. Sah, "Social Osmosis and Patterns of Crime," *Journal of Political Economy* 99, 6 (December 1991), 1272–95.

5. E. Glaeser, B. Sacerdote, and J. Scheinkman, "Crime and Social Interactions," *Quarterly Journal of Economics* 111, 2 (May, 1996), 507.

6. Harrison Hong and Marcin Kacperczyk, *The Price of Sin: The Effects of Social Norms on Markets*, working paper, Princeton University, 2006, p. 1.

7. James Altucher, "Vice Beats Virtue in the Battle for High Returns," *Financial Times*, December 18, 2006.

8. Quoted in Oliver Balch, "Raising the Bar of Performances," *Financial Times*, November 29, 2004, p.7.

9. Deutsche Presse-Agentur, "Thousands in Turin Protest Workplace Deaths," December 10, 2007.

10. AFX News, "Seventh person dies after Thyssenkrupp Italian steel mill fire," December 30, 2007, available at www.forbes.com/markets/feeds/afx/2007/12/30/afx4481614.html.

11. Quoted in "Thousands in Turin Protest Workplace Deaths," *La Republica*, December 10, 2007.

Chapter 6

1. Excerpt from a Definitive Proxy Statement (14A SEC Filing), filed by Walt Disney Company on January 11, 2006, publically available at http://sec.edgar-online.com/2006/01/11/0001193125-06-004951/Section11.asp.

2. Henry Blodget, "The Conscious Investor," *Atlantic Monthly*, October 2007.

3. If you are curious and want to check sources of pollution around your home, you can consult the Toxic Release Inventory at the website of the Environmental Protection Agency, www.epa.gov/tri/.

4. Joe Nocera, "Well-Meaning but Misguided Stock Screens," *New York Times*, April 7, 2007.

5. Blodget, p. 82.

6. Karen Damato, "Social Studies: How 'Responsible' Funds Differ on Stock Choices," Wall Street Journal (Eastern edition), May 18, 2000, p. C. 1.

INDEX